MECHANICS-
MERCANTILE
LIBRARY.

Arthur F. Mathews '06

BOOKS BY JEROME CHARYN

Savage Shorthand

The Green Lantern

Gangsters and Gold Diggers

Bronx Boy

The Isaac Quartet

Sizzling Chops and Devilish Spins

Hurricane Lady

The Black Swan

Captain Kidd

Citizen Sidel

Death of a Tango King

The Dark Lady from Belorusse

El Bronx

Little Angel Street

Montezuma's Man

Back to Bataan

Maria's Girls

Elsinore

The Good Policeman

Movieland

Paradise Man

Metropolis

War Cries Over Avenue C

Pinocchio's Nose

Panna Maria

Darlin' Bill

The Catfish Man

The Seventh Babe

Secret Isaac

The Franklin Scare

The Education of Patrick Silver

Marilyn the Wild

Blue Eyes

The Tar Baby

Eisenhower, My Eisenhower

American Scrapbook

Going to Jerusalem

The Man Who Grew Younger

On the Darkening Green

Once Upon a Droshky

SAVAGE
SHORTHAND

THE LIFE AND DEATH OF **ISAAC BABEL**

SAVAGE SHORTHAND

Jerome Charyn

 RANDOM HOUSE | NEW YORK

Published in the United States by Random House,
an imprint of The Random House Publishing Group,
a division of Random House, Inc., New York.

RANDOM HOUSE and colophon are registered
trademarks of Random House, Inc.

LIBRARY OF CONGRESS CATALOGING-IN-PUBLICATION DATA

Charyn, Jerome.
Savage shorthand : the life and death of Isaac Babel /
Jerome Charyn.
p. cm.
Includes bibliographical references and index.
ISBN 0-679-64306-0
1. Babel', I. (Isaak), 1894–1941. 2. Authors, Russian—
20th century—Biography. I. Title.
PG3476.B2Z62 2005
813'.54—dc22   2005042821

Printed in the United States of America on acid-free paper
www.atrandom.com
9 8 7 6 5 4 3 2 1
FIRST EDITION
All photographs are from the private collection of Nathalie Babel.

Book design by Barbara M. Bachman

THE AUTHOR WOULD LIKE TO THANK NATHALIE BABEL

FOR HER OWN WONDROUS ESSAYS ABOUT HER FATHER,

ESSAYS THAT HELPED ME WRITE THIS BOOK

CONTENTS

SAVAGE
SHORTHAND

INTRODUCTION: ISAAC BABEL

T'S THE ONE BOOK I HAVE TWO COPIES OF. THEY SIT
side by side. *The Collected Stories of Isaac Babel* (circa 1960),
with Milton Glaser's cover of three Cossacks on horseback
wiggling against a white background like quarks or some other
magic material suddenly visible to the eye. Glaser has caught
both the ferocity and the fragile charm of Babel, whose language
seems to slice at us while his characters float across our field of
vision. Babel is dangerous; he disturbs our dreams. He's cruel
and tender, like some kind of crazy witch. Each of his best stories—"The King" or "Di Grasso" or "Guy de Maupassant"—is
like a land mine and a lesson in writing; it explodes page after
page with a wonder that's so hard to pin down. The structure of
the stories is a very strange glass: we learn from Babel but cannot
copy him.

I've lived with him nearly all my adult life. I discovered Babel
after I'd written a novel and read Nabokov, Faulkner, Hemingway, James Joyce, Scott Fitzgerald, Jane Austen, Saul Bellow,

and Grace Paley. I was sitting with my editor in an Italian restaurant filled with mafiosi. He himself was a novelist, and every other editor in New York feared him, because he was a pirate who ransacked publishers' lists and stole authors at will. He didn't have to steal me. I was his single discovery, his one dark horse. And for a short period, just before my first novel was published, while he bickered with book clubs and lined up blurbs that he himself would write and then ask one of his stolen authors to sign, I remember having lunch with him every day of the week.

He happened to compose one of the blurbs while we were finishing our hazelnut cake (reserved for him and me) and coffee with lemon peel. "Incomparable," he scribbled on the tablecloth. "Stupendous." I was embarrassed at his flamboyance, and the liberties he took with the restaurant and its tablecloths. "Babel is the one and only writer who comes to mind."

"Couldn't you be a little less exotic? Who's this Babel?"

He revealed his disappointment by crushing the lemon peel and canceling all our other lunches. He wouldn't talk to me (or write another blurb) until I'd read Isaac Babel. I was whisked into another dimension where everything to do with my book stood still. I had a book jacket with my name on it but with the title missing. I had a photograph of me with half a face. I had the proofs of every fifth chapter. I found Babel's stories in a bookshop, but I resisted reading him until I fell upon "The King" and its perverse outlaw in orange pants who reigned over Odessa and disposed of his enemies by firing bullets into the air. He was called Benya Krik, and he was so recognizable that I suffered through palpitations of pleasure and pain.

Benya's native territory was a Jewish slum, the Moldavanka, home of gangsters and grocers and mythical draymen, a ghetto of dark streets that seemed outside ordinary time, suspended in the reader's own imagination. I'd met this Benya before, many times, in *my* Moldavanka, the East Bronx, where he was always defiant in his orange pants. He wasn't a drayman. His shoulders weren't broad, but he walked with his own marvelous ballet, giving out candy to all the kids. His nails might be dirty, his shoes unshined, but he was still a gallant. He didn't seek wealth, but a kind of feudalism, a fief that belonged to him and him alone. The grocers gave him food, and no one would dare steal a solitary fig from them. We never took our problems to the police—they were from another planet, aliens who didn't bother to understand our sins. The important thing was that our Benya with the dirty fingernails had no fear of them. He ruled even if he never got rich. He was the lord of empty space, prince of those without a language other than the glaring musicality of his orange pants. . . .

I read on and on. I found myself going back to the same stories—as if the narratives were musical compositions that one could never tire of. Repetition increased their value. Babel was involving me in merciless fairy tales that evoked the first books I'd ever read. With each dip into Babel I discovered and rediscovered reading itself.

I bought another copy, savored it, put it on my shelf. I wouldn't travel anywhere with my two Babels. I didn't want the binding to break. I knew nothing about him until I read the introduction beneath Milton Glaser's cover of the three wiggling Cossacks. Babel died in a concentration camp in 1939 or 1940, according to Lionel Trilling (he was murdered in the cellars of the Lubyanka; his executioner didn't fire into the air, like Benya Krik). "It has been said that he was arrested when Yagoda was purged, because he was having a love-affair with Yagoda's sister." I put a check near that sentence; the name Yagoda seemed poetic and sinister at the same time. And I couldn't stop thinking about Yagoda's sister. Yagoda himself was chief of the Cheka (Stalin's secret police). And I couldn't have known it then (few people did), but Trilling had the wrong police chief and the wrong relative. Babel had had an affair with Evgenia Yezhova, wife of Nikolai Yezhov, the Cheka chief who came after Yagoda. Yezhov was one of the great killers of the twentieth century, next to Stalin. And Evgenia and Babel died because of Yezhov, a little man with a limp. But I only learned that years after my original romance with Babel. . . .

My pirate of a publisher never took me back into the fold. He disclaimed me as his one dark horse. My novel appeared, but only with a minor hiccough from a book club, and no blurbs. I had my compensation: Babel. In 1937, at the height of Stalin's terror machine, with Yezhov in power, Babel was obliged to give an interview before the Soviet Writers Union. The questions asked of him were absurd. I offer one in particular: Why was Babel interested in the *exceptional?*—as if this were a crime. It was a crime under Stalin. But without the *exceptional*, we would have no Benya Krik, no stories about Babel's own ride with the Red Cavalry, no sense of a poetic, troubled language that reverberates in every direction, bathes us in the blood of verbs and nouns.

Babel had to give an answer. It was as absurd as the question, but with a little tongue of truth. Tolstoy, he said, "was able to describe what happened to him minute by minute, he remembered it all, whereas I, evidently, only have it in me to describe the most interesting five minutes I've experienced in twenty-four hours. Hence the short-story form."

And I carry Babel's "five minutes" in my head wherever I go. It has nothing to do with Tolstoy, with *War and Peace* versus *Red Cavalry*, or with large canvases versus small. Babel's "five minutes" were about creating volcanoes with each sentence, about conjunctions on the page that are closer to jazz riffs than to any writer (including Tolstoy), about a strange autobiographical journey in which Babel mingles with killers and rabbis, Cossacks and painters of icons, the beautiful wife of a Petersburg banker whose only dream is to translate Maupassant, philosophers with their eyes plucked out, Marxists with bullets wrapped in phylacteries; he takes us where we've never been and where we could never go—into the incredible lost land of art that Milton Glaser captures with his three cavaliers.

•

ACCORDING TO CYNTHIA OZICK, Babel "was devoured because he would not, could not, accommodate to falsehood." Yet his entire life is about falsehood, about evasion, about manufacturing myths. And because the simplest facts of his life are confusing—Babel loved to invent and revise his own biographical data—a chronology, with its own cast of characters, might provide a frame or a picture window through which we can observe Babel, hold him for an instant under our very own looking glass.

1894 Isaac Babel, son of Emmanuel (Manus) and Fanya
      Babel, is born in the Moldavanka, Odessa's Jewish
      quarter, on June 30. Odessa was unlike any other town
      in the Russian empire. A port on the Black Sea, it was
      flooded with foreigners, and swollen with Jews from
      the shtetls of the Ukraine, where Manus and Fanya's
      people had come from. It resembled Coney Island or
      Brighton Beach, with its parade of petty Jewish
      gangsters and shop owners by the sea. The Babels
      moved to Nikolaev, another port town on the Black
      Sea, a little after Isaac's birth.

1899 Babel's "silent sister," Maria, is born to Manus and
      Fanya in Nikolaev. She will never appear as a character
      in his fiction. But some of his most poignant letters were
      written to Maria after she moved to Brussels in 1924.

1905 One of the most turbulent years in Russian history.
      Russia is defeated by the Japanese after a short,
      humiliating war. It endures a revolution and a general
      strike, spurred on by this defeat. The tsar makes certain
      concessions in his October manifesto to the people,
      promising a constitutional monarchy. A pogrom breaks
      out in southern Russia that same October, encouraged
      by the tsar and his ministers. Russia had had a history of
      pogroms ever since the assassination of Tsar Alexander
      II. Accused of having planned Alexander's death, Jews

were attacked in over two hundred towns. The
government saw this bloodletting as a means of
controlling and "calming" the people, and would often
help choreograph the beginning *and* end of a particular
pogrom. Babel witnessed the pogrom of 1905 in
Nikolaev, during three days and nights near the end of
October. Neither he nor his family was harmed. But the
pogrom would become a powerful motif in his fiction,
and he would insinuate himself into the action as both a
sufferer and celebrant: the pogrom excited Babel,
aroused him, flooded him with language.

1906   Unable to get into a traditional gymnasium because of
the government's restrictions against Jews, even in
"Jewish" Odessa, Babel is sent to a commercial school,
Nicholas I, in 1906, and the Babels move back to
Odessa, settling in a posh part of town. It was while at
Nicholas I that he fell in love with the work of Guy de
Maupassant.

1911   Sent by his father to Kiev, where he enrolls at the
Institute of Finance and Business Studies, Babel meets
his closest "collaborator," Evgenia Gronfein, or Zhenya,
a free-spirited fifteen-year-old girl who believed in the
sanctity of art. She was the daughter of Boris Gronfein,
a rich manufacturer of agricultural machinery. Young
Isaac was welcomed into the household. Gronfein and
his wife practically adopted him, but they didn't expect

their own little princess to fall in love with a bumpkin from Odessa.

1916 Babel arrives in Petersburg, living from hand to mouth, he claims, hoping to become the Russian Maupassant. He had little luck with his stories until he met Maxim Gorky. (There was no one quite like Gorky in Russian or any other literature. He would shepherd into being— protect, nourish, provoke—an entire generation of young writers, including Babel and Yuri Olesha, author of *Envy*. He read their work, edited it before *and* after publication, marking up manuscripts and books with a big fat crayon.)

Gorky will "command" Babel to go out into the world—a dangerous proposition. Gorky hadn't been a wanderer by theory or decree. He was a hobo who sucked in his surroundings, who educated himself on the road; his tutors were fellow tramps and Volga boatmen. He was rawboned and muscular, a tall proletarian prince. And Babel was a bookworm from Odessa with weak eyes and "autumn in his heart," but his imagination was like a house on fire: his entire life seemed to be an internal dialogue with Gorky, the need to see himself as a picaro—a cavalier on his own precipitous battlefront.

1917–
1918   These two years are a kind of shadowland for Babel *and many other Russians*. He may have served in the Cheka (as a translator), may have been "a soldier on the Rumanian front," but there are few real records of Babel's activities: it's a time of upheaval—revolution and civil war—and Babel may have fallen into some historical crack where biography blends with myth.

1919   Babel marries his sweetheart from Kiev, Evgenia Gronfein (Zhenya), and lives with her in Odessa, surrounded by his sister, mother, father, uncles, nieces, aunts—a whole tribe of Babels.

1920   While in Odessa with his bride, he conspires with the local Communist Party to finagle him into General Budenny's Red Cavalry as a war correspondent under a Russian pseudonym—Kiril Lyutov. He will spend only four or five months with the Cossacks (from June to September or October 1920), but the diary he kept during his "service" with Budenny would shape him as a writer. For once, Gorky's *commandment* was correct: Babel had gone into the world and discovered a whirlwind in Poland, in the war between Cossacks and Polish cavalrymen.

1921   Babel publishes "The King," his first celebrated story.

———While Russia is ravaged by civil war, Lenin
introduces NEP (New Economic Policy), or "the
breather," a return to capitalism on a small scale. He
will allow peasant farmers to grow rich, will bring back
nightclubs and casinos, hotels and restaurants for
foreigners, even a cadre of prostitutes. Moscow has its
own Jazz Age. Experimentation flourishes in all the
arts. It is during NEP that Babel matures as a writer,
finds his own complex "music." But Lenin still means
to pounce. "It's a very great mistake to think that NEP
means the end of terror," he tells one of his
commissars, himself a terrorist. "We shall resort to
terror again."

1922   Lenin creates a new post, General Secretary of the
Party, and anoints Stalin as the first "Gensek." All of
Stalin's power will come from this post.

1922–
1923   The most fecund period in Babel's life. Part of the time
he lives with Zhenya on a mountain near Batum.
Working in isolation, with Zhenya beside him, he
completes his Odessa tales and begins the stories that
will become *Red Cavalry*.

1923 Babel's father dies in Odessa. He will miss Manus
more than he ever might have imagined. Manus had
been imposing, handsome, unpredictable, given to
sudden rages—a father who might have been invented
by Franz Kafka. But Manus had also believed in Isaac's
uniqueness, wanted him to be a prodigy on the violin,
while Fanya preferred that he not be *noticeable* in a
world that didn't look favorably upon Jews. "When I
go through moments of despair, I think of Papa," Babel
wrote to Fanya in 1927. "What he expected and
wanted of us was success not moaning. Remembering
him, I feel a surge of strength."

———Stories from *Red Cavalry* begin to appear in
print.

1924 General Semion Budenny attacks Babel, calls him an
impostor who never saw any action in the First Cavalry.
Budenny himself was one of the Revolution's strangest
characters. He was born into a family of peasants in
Cossack country, near Rostov on the Don, in 1883. As
Babel remembered him, he had dazzling white teeth.
He was also famous for his mustache, which bloomed
near his nose like a pair of horizontal trees. He served
in one of the tsar's Cossack regiments, joined the
Revolution, and was made commander-in-chief of the
Soviets' mythical troopers, the Red Cavalry. Brash,

arrogant, barely literate, he adored the Cossacks with
their bowler hats and colorful blankets, and he
despaired of Babel's book about *his* cavalry. Babel, he
believed, was a voyeur who had maligned the
Cossacks, turned them into gargoyles and goats.
Budenny was named a marshal of the Soviet Union in
1935, survived Stalin's purges, and appeared on the
cover of *Time* magazine in 1941, with his glorious
mustache. "An army as brave as its privates—but only
as good as its general," *Time*'s caption read.

———Lenin dies and the "Gensek," Joseph Stalin,
master of the Party, begins his incredible rise to power.
When Lenin's widow, Krupskaya, complains about him,
the "Gensek" tells her to shut up or he will find Lenin
another widow.

———Babel moves to Moscow with his mother, sister,
and wife. His stories bring him a sudden, immediate
fame. He finds himself "swaggering with the generals."
People in Moscow begin talking like Benya Krik. At the
end of the year, his sister, Maria, moves to Brussels to be
with her fiancé, Grisha Shapochnikoff, a medical
student. Her departure signals the breakup of his own
little family (his mother will join Maria in 1926).

1925   Zhenya leaves for France at the end of the year to study
art. Babel is ambivalent to say the least. He'd begun an

affair in Moscow with a beautiful blond actress, Tamara Kashirina.

1926　First publication of *Red Cavalry* as a book. Babel now has a new career: screenwriter. He adapts his Odessa tales into a screenplay entitled *Benya Krik*. He will continue writing screenplays for the rest of his life.

————Mikhail, Babel's child with Tamara, is born in July.

1927　Tamara soon tires of her nomad. She's particularly annoyed when Babel abandons Moscow in July to visit his wife in France. "Leave me alone and never write me again," she sang like a melancholic diva. Tamara was much too wily for Babel, much too tempestuous, and she would never have put up with his tricks. Babel liked to dissemble, Babel liked to hide. . . .

　　She will marry another Soviet writer, Vsevolod Ivanov, and forbid Babel ever to see his own little boy again.

JULY 1927–
OCTOBER 1928　Babel's first trip abroad.

————Babel has a "fling" with Evgenia Gladun (later Yezhova). Little is known about her except that she liked to collect husbands as well as lovers. She met

Babel in Berlin, while she was married to a minor diplomat, Alexander Gladun. Evgenia seemed to live for romance—she kept an apartment outside Moscow for her trysts—until she met Nikolai Yezhov (future chief of the Cheka), whom she married around 1931. She was intensely loyal to Babel, found jobs for him, and was foolish enough not to destroy his love letters to her. Yezhov was aware of these letters. He had her poisoned in 1938.

1928   Babel publishes his first play, *Sunset.*

———Stalin declares an end to NEP and begins an era of forced collectivization, the first Five-Year Plan. A creature of NEP, Babel flourished during Stalin's little "flirtation" with the West. But the regime becomes more and more repressive. Stalin will call 1929 the "year of the great breaking point." He's prepared to kill all sense of adventure—in people and in the arts.

———Babel can't seem to settle in France (he's been gone fifteen months). Celebrated in Moscow, he's utterly unknown in Paris, except among Russian émigrés. He's often ill and can't write. "I am living terribly," he will tell a friend. But Zhenya continues to love him in spite of his blond bombshell in Moscow. She will become pregnant during his last days in Paris.

1929   Their daughter, Nathalie or Natasha, is born in Paris on
July 17. Her birth will be Babel's "undoing." He longed
to be with her, but the Soviet bureaucrats wouldn't
allow him to leave the country again: the author of *Red
Cavalry* wasn't productive enough. He couldn't seem to
paint much of a picture of the Soviet "pioneers."

————Babel travels across the Ukraine and visits
collective farms, searching for new material.

1932   Babel meets Antonina Pirozhkova (born in Siberia in
1909), a young construction engineer who will help
build the Moscow metro.

SEPTEMBER 1932–
AUGUST 1933   Babel's second trip abroad. He can't really
recover from meeting his little daughter, Natasha, who'd
arrived at the age of three *without* him. He would escort
her everywhere, a prisoner to her own sense of play. But
not even Natasha can hold him in Paris. He'd received a
mysterious summons from Moscow, he told a friend.

1934   Genrikh Yagoda (born in Poland in 1891) is appointed
chief of the Cheka. It was Yagoda who helped build
some of Stalin's worst labor camps, Yagoda who had his
own poison laboratory. Babel would visit him at the
Lubyanka, the Cheka's headquarters and prison, close

to Red Square. Because of these visits, rumors began to spread that Babel was writing a novel about the Cheka. No page of this novel was ever found.

JUNE–
AUGUST 1935   Babel's third and final trip abroad. He attends an international anti-Fascist congress of writers in Paris. *Red Cavalry* has been translated into English, German, French . . . and he finds himself celebrated in France. But it's the last time he will ever see Nathalie or Zhenya. After his return to Moscow, he began living with Antonina Pirozhkova. She wasn't a diva, like Tamara Kashirina. She never badgered him, or intruded upon his privacy. She left him the space to have his own secret maneuvers, and he was always maneuvering. Even while he was living with Antonina, he dreamt of returning to France.

1936   Babel loses his one great protector when Gorky dies on June 18.

———Nikolai Yezhov (born in Lithuania in 1895) succeeds Yagoda as boss of the Cheka and becomes Stalin's chief executioner.

1937   Antonina and Babel have a daughter, Lydia, born in January; though still married to Zhenya, Babel will welcome Antonina as his second "wife."

1938   Yezhov is replaced by Lavrenti Beria, a thug from
        Stalin's native Georgia, who would kidnap fourteen-
        year-old girls and keep them on his private train.

1939   Beria has Yezhov hurled into the Lubyanka, and it's
        while being tortured that Yezhov implicates Babel in a
        plot to murder Stalin.

———Babel is arrested on May 15, a few days after
Yezhov's "confession." The Cheka seizes all his
manuscripts and seals them inside the Lubyanka.

1940   Stalin has him shot in the early morning of January 27,
        and thus begins one of the modern mysteries of Russian
        literature: Babel's death. No one but Stalin and the
        Cheka knew the details.

1944   Stalin is a bit bewildered. He can't be seen as the
        butcher of Isaac Babel, a *zhid* who might become a
        martyr in the West. After the war he sends his own spies
        to France, men and women who bump into Zhenya on
        the street, insist that Babel is still alive. Stalin didn't
        have to be quite so tender with Antonina, who was
        stuck in Moscow. He simply had the Cheka send her
        reports that Babel was in a labor camp, playing chess
        with the commandant. . . .

1953   The Boss has forgotten about Babel. He's becoming more and more paranoid. He keeps arresting Jews, and is planning to send them all to Siberia. But his madness wasn't confined to Jews. He'd gotten rid of his favorite bodyguard, and prepared to pounce on the whole Politburo. And then *his* poisoners poisoned him. He lay in his own piss for thirteen hours and not a doctor was called. Members of the Politburo came and went: Comrade Stalin, the great dictator, died like a dog.

1954   Babel's rehabilitation begins. He goes from being a nonperson to a *possible* person. A death certificate is produced, with a fanciful date—March 17, 1941— composed by the Cheka, without the slightest indication of how or where he had died. It was the usual Soviet dance: a little noise and a lot of lies . . .

1957   Zhenya Gronfein, Babel's "lost" wife, dies in Paris on May 17. She was, as her daughter suggests, a stateless person, a woman without a country who created her own little country of art. (Babel also lived in that little country—with and without his bride—and he would never recapture the creative fever he had with Zhenya in 1922, when they shared a mountain with bandits in Batum.)

1961   Babel's daughter Nathalie arrives in New York with a
        single suitcase, a winter coat on her arm, "and twenty
        dollars in my purse." She's almost as much of a picaro
        as Babel himself. She will become his most loyal editor
        in America and write a pair of feisty essays about him
        that read like a fierce dialogue with the master. In some
        magical way, Babel remains with us while Nathalie is
        alive. (One of my greatest pleasures in writing this book
        was to meet Nathalie in Washington, D.C., to discover
        Babel's own perplexities in his daughter's face.)

ISAAC BABEL AT HIS HORSE FARM IN MOLDONEVO, 1930

MINGLED BIOGRAPHIES AND
MANGLED LIVES: A FIRST GLANCE

1.

N 1955, LIONEL TRILLING published a dazzling introduction to the collected stories of Isaac Babel, a writer who'd become a ghost in his own country, his books removed from libraries, his name scratched out of encyclopedias, as if he'd never existed. Babel had written the first masterpiece of the Russian Revolution, *Red Cavalry,* a cycle of stories about Cossack horse soldiers fighting against the Poles in a brutal and bloody campaign; these stories had the "architecture" and complexity of a novel, a Cubist novel built on a wild geometry where the missing pieces were an essential part of the puzzle. Babel was idolized and attacked for the same reason: rather than celebrate the Revolution, he galloped across it with a cavalryman's panache. He was the one Soviet writer who was read abroad. That made him an infidel in the Party's eyes. And he had to walk a curious tightrope for the rest of his life—revere the Revolution and write a prickly, personal prose that was like a time bomb to the Revolution's dull, pragmatic songs.

Babel fell into silence, wandered the Soviet Union; in the few photographs we have of him, he looks like a man wearing the mask of a grocery clerk. The rebellious writer had to be hidden at all cost. And so Babel became the jovial pal of the proletariat, who'd rather talk with jockeys and whores than with a fellow writer. Whereas he'd talked about literature day and night with his first wife, Zhenya, while he was with her in Batum, would read his stories to her until they were burnt into her heart and she could recite them twenty years later, he wouldn't even show his manuscripts to his second wife, Antonina. He was practicing to become a man of the people who hung out at a stud farm, but he'd used up his own interior space. He was one of the voiceless men—"Ten steps away no one hears our speeches"—in Osip Mandelstam's poem about Stalin, a poem that got Mandelstam arrested, exiled, and killed. Babel never attacked the Kremlin's "mountaineer" with "cockroach whiskers." Stalin was one of his readers, but that couldn't save him.

He was given a dacha in the writers' colony of Peredelkino, and he disappeared from that dacha in May 1939. The secret police had moved him and his manuscripts to their own "dacha" in the middle of Moscow, otherwise known as the Lubyanka. And when Lionel Trilling wrote about him sixteen years later, his death had become only one more enigma in a land of enigmas. He'd been declared an enemy of the people, a spy for Austria, England, and France, and was finished off in 1940, shot twice in the head—the bullet holes were stuffed with rags—and cremated, his ashes emptied into a communal pit. Neither Stalin nor his Cheka bothered to tell anyone, and the myth of Babel languishing in some Siberian camp lingered for years. There were constant sightings of Babel, campmates who swore he was still alive. The Cheka itself manufactured these tales. It was imitating the artistry of Isaac Babel. . . .

By 1954, a year before Trilling's introduction, Babel was "resurrected" in the Soviet Union, pronounced a person again, though the Cheka persisted in giving him a phony death date, March 17, 1941, and wouldn't reveal how or where he had died. It was the United States that had to reinvent Babel in the person of Lionel Trilling, a godlike figure on Columbia's campus. Trilling abhorred violence. And here he was writing about Isaac Babel, the poet of violence, who touched upon a primitive, amoral madness and seemed deeply ambivalent about it.

Babel himself had been a war correspondent attached to General Budenny's First Cavalry, which consisted almost completely of Cossacks, and in a fictional rendering of his ride across Poland and the Ukraine with Budenny's troops, one can almost feel Babel imagine himself as a *little* Cossack, with more than a bit of self-mockery as he begins to imitate their own cruel creed. Readers loved the stories, which belonged to that tiny "window" during the twenties when Russia was like a Wild, Wild West with its own avant-garde in the middle of NEP (Lenin's New Economic Policy), as "beautiful women in mink coats" suddenly appeared in Moscow, some of them clutching copies of Isaac Babel. It troubled Trilling when he first read the stories in 1929. He'd been hoping that the Revolution might offer him an art with "as little ambiguity as a proposition in logic." And here was Babel, full of ambiguities.

In a 1948 essay about Huckleberry Finn, Trilling describes Huck's moral dilemma regarding Jim, the runaway slave whom he condescends to but can never seem to denounce. Huck's own heart, like Babel's, is a "battleground" of competing ideas and obligations. In a land of liars, he learns to lie. Yet whatever Huck's chicanery, we never doubt his essential goodness and his reverence for the godlike Mississippi, a river that equips him with language and a sense of wonder. But there are no river gods on the ride to Poland, only Cossacks and their rituals of slaughter.

Trilling notes Babel's "lyric joy in the midst of violence," a rhapsody that almost numbs the reader and allows Babel to detach himself from the suffering he describes. Trilling finds in this the key to Babel's art: "the apparent denial of immediate pathos is a condition of the ultimate pathos the writer conceives."

And this masked pathos is but one more enigma of Isaac Babel, the man of many masks. Babel had crept under the wing of Maxim Gorky, Russia's most revered writer, whose popularity rivaled Stalin's. Gorky had been living in Sorrento, under Mount Vesuvius, and it was Stalin who lured him back to the Soviet Union in 1932, naming streets and parks and entire cities after this writer-saint who'd risen out of the lower depths, and "crowned" him the first president of the Soviet Writers Union. Babel couldn't be harmed while Gorky was alive. In one apocryphal tale that Babel himself loved to tell, Gorky pops into the Kremlin with his protégé, has an audience with Stalin, who asks

Babel why he hasn't written a novel about Gorky's "Boss" (it was Gorky who began calling Stalin the country's "senior comrade" and "Boss"). Babel doesn't answer. He smiles. At the first Soviet Writers' Congress in 1934, attended mostly by half-men and hacks who'd sold themselves to the Soviet dogma of socialist realism, Babel stood outside this dogma, said he was the master of a new genre, the genre of silence. He praised the Boss's laconic style—sentences that had the sensation of steel. Yet there was something perverse about Babel's speech, as if he were "addressing his fellow-writers in a dead language," the dead talking to the dead in a country that sought to destroy all the idiosyncrasy of art.

Gorky died in 1936, probably poisoned by Stalin, who could no longer afford the whimsies of this old man. Stalin was bent on killing as many intellectuals as he could, and the *starik* might have used his prestige to get in the way. With Gorky gone, Babel no longer had a protector. How could the Soviets have reconciled themselves to Babel's wayward art? "Intensity, irony, and ambiguousness . . . constitute a clear threat to the impassivity of the State. They constitute a *secret.*"

And so Babel was shoved into oblivion. And I couldn't help but marvel at Trilling's devotion to Babel, who wrote about Cossacks and the Moldavanka, the Jewish slums of Odessa, which had given birth to the King, Benya Krik, Babel's most celebrated character, a gangster in orange pants—"the Jewish gangs of Odessa were famous," Trilling tells us, without realizing that it was Babel who made them famous, that the Moldavanka was a poor, pathetic slum that Babel had mythologized, that there was nothing but the remotest counterpart to Benya Krik, the Crier, who could outwit Odessa police chiefs, fall in love with a merchant's daughter during one of his night raids, and immediately return all of the merchant's goods.

Trilling was a classicist who did not believe in creativity's lower depths. He was too much of a measured man. I remember him on campus, with his silver hair and tweed vests and British diction that every English instructor adopted in the hope of cannibalizing Lionel Trilling. He was the lord of enlightenment and reason in the late 1950s, when literature still ruled the earth, and we poor undergraduates had a talmudic devotion to the writer's craft. He was much more vivid than a movie star.

He was also a novelist, a teller of tales, but his fiction was curiously cloistered and flat, as if he didn't dare to enter any wildness. "For all my life, the fear of insanity has blocked the free play of my imagination and made me too intent upon reasonableness," declares Diana Trilling, Lionel's wife, but she could have been writing about Lionel himself. It was in his essays that he paid homage to the river gods and found his own lilt—freed of creativity, he could afford to become creative. His essays were as musical as his name. He could have been writing a kind of dream-novel when he wrote about Huckleberry Finn and Isaac Babel.

And there were wicked stories about him. That he was the son of a Bronx tailor, that he himself was a child of the ghetto, that Lionel Trilling couldn't have been his real name, that he was some kind of Monte Cristo who took revenge on his own impoverished past, the Jewish Gatsby who'd become a literary critic rather than a bootlegger, and reinvented himself as an Oxford don with his own kingdom on Morningside Heights.

The don died in 1975, and pretty soon his own belief in a measured imagination seemed expendable in a world that was moving closer and closer to chaos.

And then a couple of years ago I happened upon Diana Trilling's memoir about her marriage to Lionel. And suddenly I had a different Trilling. He was indeed the son of a tailor, but a men's custom tailor who might have dressed the king of England . . . or an Oxford don, a tailor who turned to manufacturing coats for the chauffeurs of millionaires and hadn't brought up Lionel in any rough equivalent of the Moldavanka.

A bookish child who never had a bicycle or roller skates, he would become the first Jewish professor of English in the Ivy League. Even with a name that could have been invented by the master of all novelists, Henry James, Trilling had to twist himself into some kind of Anglo-Saxon golem (it was the 1930s, and the very best English departments still believed that Jews weren't refined enough to teach Shakespeare or Keats or Matthew Arnold). He suffered from long bouts of depression, saw himself as a failed writer of fiction, and must have sensed his own unlived imaginative life, the mask he had to wear as Lionel Trilling.

And perhaps this explains his attraction to Babel, and his ability to intuit the pathos beneath Babel's savage lines. Trilling must have felt an affinity with Benya Krik, that gangster in orange pants, as lyrical as language itself, a warrior with all the grace and willfulness of poetry. Trilling could have been dreaming about himself when he says of Babel: "[T]he unexpectedness which he takes to be the essence of art is that of a surprise attack." He was Babel's secret sharer, a writer who would have liked to shuck off his academic clothes and veer toward the unexpected, with its quota of surprise attacks.

2.

IN 1996 ANTONINA PIROZHKOVA, well into her eighties, published her own memoir of a marriage, *At His Side: The Last Years of Isaac Babel;* it was the reworking of a sketch written in 1972, when she had to erase all "criminal elements," including Babel's arrest (which the Soviets still didn't like to acknowledge), as if the author of *Red Cavalry* had died in bed, or had never died at all. *The Last Years of Isaac Babel* is a curious, almost neutral text. It seems to lack what Emily Dickinson called "a certain slant of light"—an opening, a signature, a point of view. It's a memoir in search of a voice, without the least bit of persona. "Lionel taught me to think; I taught him to write," declares Diana Trilling, and we never mistake her own presence in the marriage or in the memoir, where she claims her own territory as a writer, next to Lionel Trilling, but Antonina doesn't see herself as a writer, only as Babel's handmaiden.

We discover details about Isaac, that he loved to fondle a piece of string while he wrote, that he was a prodigious tea drinker, that he would pretend to be a woman if he really didn't want to answer the phone, and that he had a ruinous generosity: "Babel's kindness bordered on the catastrophic. . . . He would give away his watch, his shirts, his ties, saying: 'If I want possessions, it's only so that I can give them away.' "

Babel "believed that people were born for merriment," but how much merriment could there have been by the mid-thirties, when Stalin began to crush every single independent voice around him? It's to another writer, Ilya Ehrenburg, that Babel confesses: "Today a man only talks freely with his wife—at night, with the blankets pulled over his head." But we don't get much of this world under the covers from Antonina, or the crippling pain that Babel must have had about his own inability to produce under Stalin's reign of terror, when no one's wild geometry would have been welcomed. . . .

In 1935–1936, Babel collaborated with Sergei Eisenstein on *Bezhin Meadow*, a film about Pavlik Morozov, a young Soviet "Pioneer" killed by the kulaks (rich peasant farmers) after denouncing his own dad as a hoarder of grain. Stalin encouraged a Pavlik cult, and statues of Pavlik Morozov sprang up in the remotest places. He'd become the little secular saint of the Soviet Union. Antonina had gone to Yalta with Babel and "Eisen" while they worked on *Bezhin Meadow*. And Antonina allows us a tiny glimpse into Eisenstein's metaphysics. Eisen wanted to film the little saint wandering through a wheat field, wounded, and wearing a halo around his head. "Eisen," Babel said, "has told me many times he prefers what isn't there to actuality—the *isn't-ness*."

Isn'tness was the invisible border of Eisenstein's (and Babel's) art, that violent rendering of a strange new reality that came from the clash of images. Babel had practiced his own kind of cinematic crosscutting in *Red Cavalry*—the bump of invisible borders, where epiphanies could collide with the commonplace, Cossacks in bloodred boots lost in a land of poor, disheveled Polish Jews.

Antonina was right there with two of Russia's greatest stylists working on a mad Stalinian project, the *pietà* of Pavlik Morozov, and all she can tell us about the collaboration is that Babel hid Eisen's obscene doodles from her. It's as if Babel inhabited some strange shadowland while he was alive: "endowed with great goodness of spirit," he remains as unreal as . . . Pavlik Morozov. She's guarded his intimacy to such a degree, she can't bring herself to reveal whatever flaws he might have had. All we ever get about his writer's life is a piece of string, and not the perverse details of what it must have been like to dangle under Stalin's thumb, to live as a celebrated writer—worshipers would demand his autograph and Eisen's at whatever restaurant they went—who could only practice his craft in some subterranean way.

Fear of Hitler saved Eisenstein from the firing squad. It was 1937, and Stalin needed an epic that would unite the Soviet people. He put Eisenstein to work *rebuilding* Alexander Nevsky, a thirteenth-century prince whose peasant army defeated the Teutonic Knights on a battlefield of ice. *Nevsky* was an enormous hit. After the release of the film, there was a run on paper clips. "Children have been buying boxes of paper clips by the dozen to make chain mail as worn" by the prince. Eisen's film was a fable of Stalin himself, the people's prince who kept a primitive Russia from falling into chaos. But Babel had no princes in chain mail. He could only deliver Odessa and Benya Krik.

Once Babel himself is delivered to the Cheka and vanishes from Antonina's life, the neutral tone of the memoir begins to lift. Suddenly he's much more present in the book. She's no longer a passive spider in the house of Isaac Babel. She becomes a tainted person, the wife of an enemy of the people. "After Babel's arrest, no one telephoned me any longer." Once a month, she would go to a small window near Moscow's Kuznets Bridge and drop off seventy-five rubles for Babel, who wasn't allowed any visitors. And she had her own odd dance with the same Cheka that "sealed Babel's room, took away his manuscripts, diaries, and pages with signed dedications that had been torn from his books."

Babel's publishers began to "attack" Antonina, trying to retrieve the advances they had paid Babel for books he'd never delivered. And when court officials showed up at her flat and began to count not only furniture "but even my dresses," Antonina called the Cheka. A voice at the other end of the line guaranteed her that no one would come to count furniture again. And no one ever did.

When rugs were stolen from Babel's vacant dacha, it was the Cheka that helped her navigate the whirlpool between local militia and the thieves themselves. And five months after Babel's arrest, a young Chekist dropped in to collect "trousers, socks, and

handkerchiefs for Babel." Antonina scented the handkerchiefs
"heavily" with her own perfume. "I so much wanted to send
Babel a greeting from home, even if it was just a familiar scent."

These scented handkerchiefs are the most intimate detail in
the book, and they disturb our psyche as we imagine how much
Babel, a prisoner of the State, had to pull from so little, how the
artifacts of his life had been narrowed down to a trace of perfume, the last semblance of sanity in a world where, deprived of
his eyeglasses and his belt, he had to grope around half-blind
and clutch at his pants, confessing to crimes he couldn't have
committed, so that Antonina and their little daughter, Lydia
(born in 1937), wouldn't be touched.

In 1940 she was told by one of the military prosecutors that
Babel had been sentenced to ten years without the right of correspondence, which meant in the Cheka's coded language that
Babel was already dead, but Antonina didn't have the means of
breaking this code, and she continued to believe that he was at
some camp. She would make yearly inquiries, and the same curt
note would come back from the Cheka: "Alive and well in the
camps." The secret police began sending ex-cons or *zeks* to Antonina with tales of having come across Babel in their travels
from camp to camp. An elaborate fiction was woven right around
her.

Antonina was given her own godfather, Y. E. Elsberg, an editor at a Moscow publishing house whose specialty was spying
on writers. Even before Babel's arrest, Elsberg had been Antonina's helpmate. "If I mentioned that a plug had gone bad, an
electrician would show up the very next day." He would escort

Antonina to the Bolshoi, bring her a bag of oranges before the intermission, take her home "in a stylish black car." And while Babel sat in the Lubyanka, Elsberg "would come by all dressed up like a suitor," with gifts for Antonina's little girl. . . . Antonina was allowed to live in Babel's flat, but a Cheka magistrate moved into Babel's "sealed room" and sat for seventeen years without a single book, like some nagging devil put there to taunt Antonina. Babel's comrades from the Writers Union were even worse than this demon. They began to fight over Babel's dacha within a month of his arrest. . . .

There was a "thaw" in the affairs of renegade writers, dead or alive, after Stalin's own death in 1953, and the case against Babel was dismissed, but Antonina still couldn't get much out of the Cheka. Babel's death certificate read:

PLACE OF DEATH—Z; CAUSE—Z.

In 1955 one of Babel's fellow writers, whom Antonina calls K, told her that his own father, who'd been the warden at a certain Siberian camp, had once befriended Babel. The prisoners "made Babel a dark-green canvas cloak, which he wore regularly. . . . Babel had his own room in this camp; they did not force him to work, so he was able to write."

According to K, Babel's cell was next to the warden's quarters, with a common balcony. "K's mother would make meat dumplings for Babel." And it was on the warden's "black vinyl sofa that Babel had died of a heart attack."

We begin to wonder about this monstrous fabulation, this assembly of lies, as if the Cheka's central concern was the spinning out of myth within their private matrix, where reality could be qualified according to their own wish. These lies had little to do with Babel. The machine just couldn't stop. It had to blunt and obscure the simple fact that Babel had died for nothing, that his imprisonment was a theater piece staged for Stalin (the Boss was aware of every single arrest).

But Antonina had her own fierce will. She labored to get Babel's work republished "in his native land." It wasn't until 1990 that a "complete" edition appeared. I met Antonina in Paris around this time. It was at some seminar devoted to Babel. I remember a woman with a gorgeous smile that not even Stalin and his Cheka could corrupt. She wasn't a poetess or a literary critic who kept the cadence of Babel's stories inside her head. She was an engineer who was building a new kind of subway out of Babel's books, a subway of readers. Babel had badly needed an engineer like her to forage in a bewildering bureaucracy of publishers and unearth diaries and stories that had been squirreled away in some city where Babel had once toiled as a screenwriter or a journalist, writing in a secret little room that the Cheka had never known about; he adored such closets. I told her in the little Russian I had left from graduate school that Babel was a writer I adored. The beautiful Antonina blushed, and her eyes ripped with delight; her love of Babel was much larger than any Soviet myth machine.

Chapter One

THE HEADLESS MAN

1.

KONSTANTIN PAUSTOVSKY (1892–1968), one of the rare Soviet writers who survived Stalin's purges, Stalin's Red Death, met Babel in 1921, right after the publication of "Korol" ("The King") in *The Sailor*, an Odessa magazine. It was the first of Babel's Benya Krik stories, devoted to the Jewish gangsters of the Moldavanka, with their "Breughel-like bulk and brawn." "The King" created quite a stir in Odessa. Paustovsky, who lived there at the time, found himself among the Babel worshipers: "Ever since my schooldays the work of certain writers had seemed to me a form of magic. When I read 'The King' I realized that a new magician had joined the ranks."

Paustovsky knew nothing of Babel's ambience, or the aromas of Benya Krik. "The characters, their motives, their circumstances and their vivid, forceful talk—all were strange to us." Yet suddenly he was an expert on the Moldavanka, with its "population of two thousand bandits and thieves," as if Odessa were another Baghdad, with its own Ali Baba. Paustovsky wasn't even conscious of how Babel had reinvented Odessa for him, fabulated a world of banditry. He'd fallen under the magician's spell.

Babel's reputation had arrived in Odessa even before "The King." He was Gorky's protégé, just back from the Red Cavalry campaigns, "and shared in their legend," like some wild horseman of the imagination who rode with the Cossacks. But "The King" had given him local color, fixed him forever as the native son who was himself some kind of king, a king with acolytes. "Swarming round him like midges were the 'Odessa literary boys' [*literaturnye malchiki*]. They caught his jokes in midair, flew around the town with them, and ran his countless errands without complaining."

Meanwhile Babel talked and talked to Paustovsky—about love, art, his life among gangsters in the Moldavanka; about Guy de Maupassant. "He went on to tell us of his visit to Maupassant's last flat in Paris—the sun-warmed frilly pink lampshades, like the underclothes of expensive courtesans, the smell of brilliantine and coffee, and the vast rooms which frightened the sick author, who for years had schooled himself" on Maupassant.

"Babel recalled with delight the Paris he had known. He had an excellent French accent." But the accent hadn't come from any visit to Maupassant's rooms. It had come from a certain Monsieur Vadon, Babel's French teacher at the Nicholas I Commercial School, who instilled in a dreamy, nervous, nearsighted boy a lifelong love of France. And perhaps the image of lampshades like a courtesan's underpants had come from Vadon himself. Babel may have cavorted with the Red Cavalry, but he'd never been to Paris. . . .

2.

HE SUFFERED FROM mytholepsy, the maddening need to narratize oneself. It would plague him continually, so that it was impossible to tell where the myth of Babel ended and where Babel began. Like many Odessans, he loved to tell a tall tale. In 1924, as his fame grew and grew—the local hero was now the lion of Moscow—he published a terse, two-page *Avtobiographiya* peppered with half-truths, mystifications, and outright lies.

"I was born in 1894 in Odessa in the Moldavanka district," Babel begins, neglecting to remind us that his family moved to Nikolaev, a little seaport eighty miles from Odessa, when he was still an infant, and that he didn't grow up in the Moldavanka, among gangsters and horse carters who could split a man's skull with their hands. Babel's childhood was decidedly middle-class. He wasn't the son of a shopkeeper, as he would have us believe. His father sold agricultural machinery and was rich enough to afford a garden, a dovecote for young Isaac, and a yard that could double during winters as an ice-skating rink.

Next he describes his own Herculean tasks as a student. "My father insisted that I study Hebrew, the Bible, and the Talmud until I was sixteen. My life at home was hard because from morning to night they forced me to study a great many subjects. I rested at school," he says in marvelous hyperbole, a sign of his best fiction. Who else but Isaac Babel could have rested at school?

He describes his stay at the commercial school, which he entered in 1906, when his family moved back to Odessa, settling on "one of the prettiest" streets in town. "Between classes we used to go off to the jetty at the port, to Greek coffee houses to play billiards, or to the Moldavanka to drink cheap Bessarabian wine in the taverns," like some young Benya Krik preparing for adventure and a life of crime. But Lev Nikulin, his classmate at Nicholas I, who would become a lifelong friend, remembers a much different Babel, a shy, bespectacled boy in a battered cap.

Babel paints a more "truthful" picture in one of his stories ("In the Basement"), where he says: "I was an untruthful little boy. It was because of my reading: my imagination was always working overtime. . . . My nose buried in a book, I let slide everything that really mattered, such as playing truant in the harbor, learning the art of billiards in the coffeehouses on Greek Street, going swimming at Lageron," a beach in Odessa.

The *Avtobiographiya* also mentions Monsieur Vadon, who "like all Frenchmen, possessed a literary gift. . . . At the age of fifteen I began to write stories in French. I gave this up after two years; my peasant characters and my various reflections as an author turned out to be colorless." He was trying to mimic Maupassant, whose phrases Monsieur Vadon must have lovingly drummed into his head. His obsession with Maupassant would remain with him for life. But why Maupassant, who had a simple, unadorned style that wasn't the least bit *Babelesque*? Could it have been the romance of language itself? Babel had discovered French *through* Guy de Maupassant. And French was the language of Russia's royal court, woven right into the fabric of *War and Peace*. How daring it must have seemed for a boy from the provinces, a Jewish boy in a battered cap, who couldn't get into an official gymnasium despite all the Russian history and Russian verses he'd swallowed, and had to be satisfied with Nicholas I, the haven of halfwits, assorted black sheep, and pariahs like himself. And didn't he find a language that was much more regal than Russian, a language he hoped to master, like a little Guy de Maupassant?

I suspect that his "stories" in French were pastiches of Maupassant, a kind of revenge on Russia and the gymnasium that would not have him. And finally, when he did start to write in Russian, wasn't it almost like a "foreign" language for someone who'd heard his parents prattle in Yiddish at home, who would spend the last evenings at his dacha in Peredelkino before his arrest reading Sholom Aleichem in "our highly original tongue" and translating Aleichem's stories "to feed his soul"? This is not to say that Babel was a *Yiddish* writer, or that he knew Yiddish more profoundly than Russian, but it was the language of his grandparents as well as the coded tongue of the Moldavanka, which would serve as a separate kingdom to the boy and the writer he became. While his mother and sister went to Belgium, his first wife to France—"Babel clung to Moscow, hotly wed to his truest bride, the Russian language," says Cynthia Ozick. But an ambiguous bride, whom he would betray with his propaganda pieces for the Red Army and the Soviet Writers Union, and whom he would have to court in silence when Stalin's own mammoth propaganda machine began to betray him. But in his best work—*Red Cavalry, Odessa Tales,* and the stories of his childhood—Babel reaches toward a musical register we would never hear again.

The pyrotechnics that distinguish Babel are part of a metalanguage, the desire to create his own Russian, a lingua with a private glossary and stamp. And his swift, saberlike sentences seem prepared to destroy the very syntax and grammar of traditional Russian. He speaks to us in a voice that grows more and more modern, that ripples right off the edge of our new mad century, where languages can change and multiply overnight, and the ambiguous killing fields of *Red Cavalry* are suddenly as familiar as the slaughter we find on CNN.

Yet Babel wasn't being subversive in his little autobiography, modeled on Maxim Gorky. Gorky was one of the barefoot boys—*boryaki*—who'd risen out of nowhere, without education or ancestors, whose "university" had been the railroad car, the river, and the open road, and who had the popularity of a movie star *before* there were movie stars, swaying readers with his rough riverman's prose in which charismatic devils argue with God day after day. He was the number one citizen of the new Soviet state, even if he lived in self-imposed exile, a revolutionary who couldn't leave his mansion in Sorrento without being mobbed. . . .

But Gorky was in Petersburg in 1916, editing a magazine called *Letopis* ("The Chronicle"), when Babel met him. "I didn't have a residence permit, and had to avoid the police, living on Pushkin Street in a cellar rented from a bedraggled, drunken waiter." But he was far from penniless—his father continued to support him—and he was still going to school (studying law at a psychoneurological institute), which means he had much more "legality" than he was willing to admit. But the neurological institute was just a ruse. He was in Petersburg to prepare himself as a writer and to "breathe" Pushkin and Dostoyevsky and Gogol.

Editors threw him out of their offices, and he wandered like a pirate into the arms of Maxim Gorky; it was Gorky who told him that his "two or three tolerable attempts" at literature were "successful by accident," and sent him out into the world—*v lyudi*.

And now comes the biggest fable of them all. "For seven years—from 1917 to 1924—I was out in the world," a barefoot boy who became a soldier on the Rumanian front, a member of the Cheka (Babel's first wife called this a piece of pure fiction), a reporter in Tiflis, something of an apparatchik in Odessa, and more. "Only in 1923 did I learn how to express my thoughts clearly and concisely. Then I set about writing again."

So says Isaac Babel, who'd published "The King" and another Benya Krik story in 1921. The fact is, Babel had been writing all along; he took his manuscripts wherever he went, even as he was galloping into Poland, and was in constant dread of losing them. But Babel considered that his "literary career" started in 1924, when "The King" was republished in *Lef*, the most perceptive Russian journal of the period.

Babel was constructing his own chronology: the barefoot boy who followed Gorky's assignment—*komandiyorka*—and wandered across Russia as a vagabond soldier-poet and secret policeman, sucking in experience like some talented anteater, the way Gorky might have done, all the while wrestling with God and the devil. But Babel wrestled with words. He lived in a much more abstract universe than Maxim Gorky. He was constantly curious. He would meet a prostitute in Paris (long after his lies to Paustovsky) and pay her to show him the contents of her purse.

"You are a born intelligence man," Gorky once told him. "It's terrifying to let you in the door." This must have delighted Babel, who was much more complicated and perverse than the original barefoot boy. And we have to wonder about his autobiography. Was it simple performance, the need to "polish" himself and invent a persona for his Soviet masters? To cast himself as another Gorky, with working-class roots, whose own vagabondage had shaped him as a writer and a socialist? Perhaps. Gorky was the very best card he could play. But Babel's autobiography was more than an artful dodge and a confidence game. It was the attempt of a mytholept to offer himself another start, put forward an apprenticeship of seven years, yet leave out his marriage to Zhenya Gronfein in 1919, forget the little king of Odessa who gave birth to Benya Krik in 1921, forget the birth of his sister Meri, or Maria, in 1899, forget his ten or eleven years in Nikolaev, or the affection that his "Jewish shopkeeper" father had for him, and his own affection for Emmanuel (Manus) Babel, and the Dickensian list of characters that people his stories, disturbing and delighting Babel the boy. He had room for only one parent in his autobiography: Maxim Gorky. Everything else seems to disappear from Babel's portrait of the artist.

3.

BABEL DIDN'T SPRING full-grown out of the Moldavanka. He didn't spring out of the Moldavanka at all. But we have few witnesses to his boyhood and young manhood—his sister, who never appears in his stories, and whose totem name serves as the title of his second play, *Maria* (a character we never meet); a few friends and classmates like Lev Nikulin; Zhenya Gronfein, the invisible wife, and their daughter, Nathalie, or Natasha, who knew her father only as a visiting shadow when she was a little girl. And then there's the main witness, Isaac Babel, with his stories, letters, plays, propaganda, wartime diaries, speeches, interviews, and conversations that often contradict and confuse, even as they beguile. . . .

Babel was about camouflage, about the armor he wore beneath his eyeglasses—a Don Quixote on horseback, gregarious *and* withdrawn, gargantuan *and* lilliputian at the same time. Patricia Carden, who wrote one of the first books on Babel, believes that "it was in the peculiar insular world of his own mind that Babel's deepest and truest life was lived. This fact constitutes the enigma that all who knew him felt, the mystery of the other, hidden life. The works are messages to us from that other life, the only record that we have."

But Babel's works are often as bewildering as the man; his narrators are *always* unreliable, and at least in *Red Cavalry* the narration itself is close to schizophrenia. So who the hell was Isaac Babel, and what can we reliably say about him? Very little. He was born in Odessa. His mother taught him to read, according to Maria. He could be taciturn or explode into cheerfulness, and loved to play tricks on people, according to Nikulin.

His parents were also from Odessa, a city of sailors, foreigners, convicts, and Jews, founded by Catherine the Great. A seaport far from Moscow and Petersburg, Odessa enjoyed a period of relative enlightenment and prosperity for Jews. Isaac's father, Manus, was part of this prosperity: he had his own warehouse. The boy's mother, Fanya, would mock her husband's interest in wealth, in worldly things. Manus was a bold man *and* a dreamer who could fall into a terrible rage; unlike little Isaac, a runt with myopia, he had an overpowering physical presence, and wanted to make some kind of Jewish prince out of his son, a prince who would conquer the entire planet. But his wife demanded much less. She preferred that "Issya" stay at home. And she would fight with Manus over his ambitions for the boy.

Issya attended a commercial school when he couldn't get into the gymnasium, and in some way suffered through the pogrom of 1905 in Nikolaev, though he himself and his immediate family were never harmed. This pogrom is the defining motif of two tales, "The Story of My Dovecot" and "First Love." In the former, we meet him as a little boy in Nikolaev studying for the entrance exam to the gymnasium. It's hellish work—only two out of forty Jewish kids will get in. But Manus promises him a dovecote as a reward. "Never in my life have I wanted a thing more." He passes the exam, finds himself at the head of the class. Yet this isn't good enough. Khariton Efrussi, a Jewish corn and wheat baron, bribes the boy's professors, permitting Efrussi Junior to enter the gymnasium by climbing right over young Babel's back.

Manus wants to beat up the corn baron, and the boy has to return to his books and study for the next entrance exam, at which he recites Pushkin on the subject of Peter the Great and is given "an unrivaled A+."

He gets his dovecote and goes to the bird market to buy some pigeons. But he's caught in the middle of a pogrom. Makarenko, a legless cripple who rides across Odessa in a wheelchair selling cigarettes, suddenly turns on him, takes one of the "cherry-colored she-birds" and slaps him over the head with it, while Makarenko's wife shrieks about the Jews of Nikolaev. "Their spawn must be wiped out," she says.

Young Babel sits on the ground, the bird's guts trickling down his temple, blinding him in one eye. He closes his other eye. "This world was tiny, and it was awful." And in a bitter parody of David and Goliath, he opens his unstopped eye and sees a stone in front of him, "a little stone so chipped as to resemble the face of an old woman with a large jaw," just like Goliath. "A piece of string lay not far away, and a bunch of feathers that still breathed."

But he does have a curious consolation. One of the town Goliaths smashes a window frame of Khariton Efrussi's mansion, "with the amiable grin of drunkenness, sweat, and spiritual power," almost as if the mob were obeying young Babel's deepest wish.

Both his parents escape the pogrom, hiding in the home of the tax inspector, while the half-blind boy swims along with the looters, his face covered with feathers and blood. But in "First Love," the boy, with his sexuality awakened by the young wife of an army officer, watches his father being humiliated by a Cossack captain with lemon-colored gloves. Manus is trying to save his store from the "mob of hired murderers."

Galina, the young wife, washes the feathers and blood off the boy's face—he's just returned from his encounter with Makarenko—calls him a little rabbi, and says that he looks like a bridegroom now that his face is clean. He imagines himself to be a member of the Jewish Defense Corps, like the coalman's son, fighting off the mob of murderers. But the boy has a strange attack of the hiccups, which is later diagnosed as a nervous disorder, and the entire family moves back to Odessa so that the boy can have his pick of specialists.

How wise it would be to count the ways in which that pogrom marked Babel's life. Wherever he was during the pogrom—on the moon, at school, in some safe house with his pigeons—the two stories give us a jolt that's hard to ignore. The pogrom winds around the boy with such ferocious ambiguity that we can't help but read it as a focal point of his fiction. The pogrom punishes him and rewards him. Efrussi's mansion is attacked as well as

Manus' store. And if he hadn't been sullied by the cigarette boy, would he have been able to lean against Galina's hip, "her hip that moved and breathed," and would she have washed off the "smear of pigeon" sticking to his cheek like sexual matter, and kissed him on the mouth? It's as if the pogrom itself had aroused him, and sexuality is seen as a form of violence, with the Cossack officer riding as erect as a penis with "a tall peaked cap." Unable to unravel his own crisis of pleasure and pain, the reality that he's been eroticized by the pogrom, he develops a nervous disorder that covers up his confusion and guilt.

4.

"IN THE BASEMENT," the third story about his childhood, finds him a boy of twelve living with Aunt Babka, Uncle Simon, and Grandfather Leivi-Itzkhok in a basement of the Molda-vanka. Leivi-Itzkhok, an ex-rabbi who is out of his mind, was expelled from his little town for being a forger, and so young Babel has a criminal in the house. Grandfather has been scribbling a book, *The Headless Man,* on sheets of paper "as large as maps." The book describes all the neighbors he ever had—cooks at cir-cumcision parties, gravediggers, cantors, and other madmen like himself. And Uncle Simon is even worse. He loves to brag and boast about imaginary conquests. "Though to tell the truth," the boy says, "if you go by the heart, it wasn't all that untrue."

And this could be the parabola of Babel's own fiction—the pith of a story comes from the heart's particular truth, which is often hidden and full of strange trajectories and opposing signs, frustrating all those who want to find in Babel little lesson plans on good and evil. . . .

Mark Borgman, the top student at young Babel's school, tries to tell the other boys about the Spanish Inquisition. But "there was no poetry in what he said," nothing but "a mumble of long words." Young Babel, a "forger" of words like his grandfather, has to butt in. He talks about "old Amsterdam, the twilight of the ghetto, the philosophers who cut diamonds. . . . My imagination heightened the drama, altered the endings, made the beginnings more mysteriously involved," the way a storyteller should. "The death of Spinoza, his free and lonely death, appeared to me like a battle." Was Babel anticipating his own death in a regime already suspicious of the diamonds *he* could cut? How will we ever know?

In the next story, "Awakening," young Babel is now fourteen. But he finds no solace. His father tries to pass him off as an eight-year-old dwarf. Odessa was the land of infant Jewish prodigies during Babel's childhood, virtuosos on the violin. Babel mentions Jascha Heifetz and Mischa Elman, "exempted by the Tsar himself from military service," which was rather ironic, since throughout the nineteenth century Jewish boys from the age of twelve could be kidnapped from their villages and forced to serve in the tsar's army for a minimum of twenty-five years; very few of these "dwarfs" ever came back. . . .

Manus dreams of Mischa Elman's mansions and sees the family's salvation in having the boy become a little maestro. His teacher is Mr. Zagursky, a man with frail legs and a factory of Jewish dwarfs. Babel didn't have to invent his own tortured life as a false prodigy. He did suffer through the delirium of being a musical dwarf. In the letters he wrote to his mother and Maria, he talks about Zagursky's actual counterpart, Pyotr Salomonovich Stolyarsky, who still had his famous factory in 1935. Babel had watched the most recent dwarfs perform at a concert in Moscow. "We met in the foyer and fell into each other's arms. . . . Just as before, Stolyarsky is mass-producing child prodigies and supplies violinists for the concert halls of the world. I am the only one he cannot boast about. He remembered everything—our dining room, our courtyard on Tiraspolskaya Street and my determined resistance."

And with Pyotr Salomonovich in our sights, we can find in "Awakening" one of the catapults of Babel's fiction—a real event multiplied out of proportion, as "a lad suffering from hysteria and headaches" would see it. Babel has *narratized* his own life, taking whatever incident—music lessons or a pogrom—and weaving it into myth and private enigma.

In *The Wound and the Bow*, Edmund Wilson writes about the damage done to Dickens when he was twelve. His father was thrown into debtor's prison. The boy was taken out of school and obliged to work as some kind of cellar rat for six months in a blacking factory. And Wilson believes that Dickens' entire career as a writer was an attempt to "digest" these six months, which he never could:

"For the man of spirit whose childhood has been crushed by the cruelty of organized society, one of two attitudes is natural: that of the criminal or that of the rebel. Charles Dickens, in imagination, was to play the rôle of both, and to continue up to his death to put into them all that was most passionate in his feeling."

I wish I could say that Babel was a "criminal" and a "rebel" in his own mind, that the pogrom in Nikolaev—sanctioned and aided by the tsar and his police—was as big a "wound" as the blacking factory was to Dickens. The pogrom lasted three days and must have disturbed a boy who saw himself as an enlightened creature in an enlightened town, where Jews could mingle a bit more freely than in other parts of the Russian empire, become bankers, salesmen, and artists, even dare to write in the language of Tolstoy. But it didn't give him a murderous imagination. He was, as he said, an hysterical boy, prone to nervous disorders, a storyteller wrapped in multiple masks, dueling with words. Sensitive, myopic, and small. And the pogrom, however painful, would feed his imagination. He would store it in his memory, internalize it like some wily cannibal, play it upon the registers of his own past. His grandfather, "who went cracked as he grew old," spent his whole life writing *The Headless Man*. And as Babel himself says: "I took after him."

But there was yet another Headless Man, Manus, who was a writer as well as a middle-class merchant. In his spare time he would scribble out tiny satirical texts, ridiculing the vanity of neighbors and friends. Manus was mercurial and melancholy, believed that his only son could rise in an altogether Russian world. And "Awakening" relives this essential truth—Manus' megalomania about his son, and the boy's rebellion. Isaac flees from his music lessons, and when Manus finds out, Isaac locks himself inside the privy. Manus wails and hurls himself against the privy door. And he says, *almost* like a Cossack: "I am an officer. I go hunting. I'll kill him. This is the end."

But Manus' own mother saves young Isaac. "I do not wish to see blood in our house."

The boy dreams of running away, but like Babel himself—man and writer—he's "married" to Manus, feels a sympathy for him that's like a mourner's music. The stories about his childhood were written after Manus' death in 1923. Manus haunts these stories even when he doesn't appear. And didn't Isaac become a "Jewish dwarf," fiddling with language like the greatest of virtuosos? Manus was his real music teacher.

5.

"A GRACELESS, PUFFY-CHEEKED young provincial" of sixteen, he landed in Kiev in 1911, sent there by his father to enroll at the Institute of Finance and Business Studies, because as a *zhid* he was locked out of the University of Odessa. Once in Kiev, he was introduced to Boris Gronfein, a rich manufacturer of agricultural machinery who'd been doing business with Manus and considered him a friend. Gronfein was "a cultured, indulgent, generous man" with a melancholy wife, Berta Davidovna, who loved to play chess.

The Gronfeins' fifteen-year-old daughter, Zhenya, was much more sophisticated than Babel. But she still led a cloistered life.

"Great Russian literature, the Italian renaissance [...] and Balzac were more familiar and less disturbing to her than the outside world." From the moment they met, Babel and Zhenya seemed to form their own pact. "My mother and father, from adolescence on, shared a commitment to art and a belief that they ought to sacrifice everything for it," writes Nathalie Babel.

Nathalie's parents "were determined to live heroically. My mother refused to wear furs and pretty dresses her parents gave her. My father, to harden himself, would walk bareheaded in the dead of winter without an overcoat." And when Babel took Zhenya out to tea for the first time, he was no longer the shy bumpkin who refused everything the Gronfeins put before him. He began to gobble cake after cake. "When I start eating cake, I can't stop. So it's better for me not to start at all."

Babel loved to spread the rumor that Gronfein didn't like him and wouldn't accept such a raggedy boy as a son-in-law, that he had to elope to Odessa with his bride in 1919. And Paustovsky tells the story that Babel told him. "There could be no question of marriage: a penniless student, [...] Babel was not a suitable match for Gronfein's heiress."

Paustovsky continues Babel's fable. "Mama weeps into ten handkerchiefs," and Babel "is driven from the house." Paustovsky even has Berta Davidovna arrive "unannounced" in Odessa to make peace with Babel.

But something nagged at me. I was haunted by Gronfein and his poor wife, Berta Davidovna, she who boiled eggs for Babel in Odessa while Gronfein fumed in Kiev. "Gronfein cursed the Babels to the tenth generation, and disinherited his daughter." I didn't believe it. The Headless Man had transmogrified Boris and Berta Davidovna into his very own gargoyles, and had passed on his fictional dance to Paustovsky. And so I went to the "source," not Babel scholars or biographical dictionaries, but his daughter Nathalie, who might tell me the stories she'd heard from her own mother about Boris and Berta. I called her in Washington, D.C., where she was currently living—Nathalie was as much of a wanderer as the Headless Man. It was a day after the big blackout of 2003, when a whole slab of the continent from Canada to Cleveland had gone off the electrical grid, and I'd scratched half a page of this book under the myopic yellow beam of my flashlight.

"Did you have any food in the house?" Nathalie asked.

But I wanted to talk about Babel. "Gronfein and his wife couldn't have blocked the marriage, but were they happy about having Babel as a son-in-law?"

"They were not very enthusiastic."

And to get even, Babel had manufactured his own fairy tale about grabbing Zhenya away from Gronfein like some mountain chief.

"There were never any clashes," Nathalie said. "Mother adored her father," but her own mother was deeply depressed. Zhenya hadn't been the youngest child. There was another daughter, Marusia, who died at ten, before Babel got to Kiev. And after Marusia disappeared, Berta "sank into a depression that she never came out of."

She had one solace—her son Lev (Lyova), a "golden boy" and ne'er-do-well who left for the United States in 1919. Gronfein gave him a belt filled with gold coins as his final legacy from a Soviet Union that had stripped him of his means.

The gold coins must have gone to his head. I imagined Lyova squandering millions in Manhattan while he danced cheek to cheek with Zelda Fitzgerald. "He was a ladies' man," Nathalie said. "I'm told he was very handsome. He did become wealthy, but he lost everything, started all over again, and at the end of his life he had nothing."

And it's much more than a coincidence that "Lyovka" is Benya Krik's younger brother in *Sunset*, Babel's first play. Lyovka is the closest thing to a Cossack, a horse soldier on leave from the tsar's own cavalry. "A Jew who climbs onto a horse stops being a Jew and becomes a Russian," Lyovka says at the beginning of the play. And Benya's father, Mendel Krik, still king of the horse carters at sixty-two, happens to fall in love with a twenty-year-old beauty named Marusia and is willing to run off to Bessarabia and ruin his family over her. It seems as if all of Babel's fiction is derived from one continuous family, his own. . . .

Zhenya loved to reminisce about her father. Gronfein was fearless. "He would put his passport in his pocket and travel throughout Europe" without ever showing it to a single border guard, "at a time when you needed a visa to go around the corner."

But he didn't travel much after the Revolution. "He lost everything and was made the concierge of his own building"—a *dvornik.* He managed to save a string of pearls—"real pearls. And in those days," Nathalie reminded me, "duchesses and tsarinas always had pearls down to their knees."

And Babel's own pearls, pearls that he hid? He lived inside language, lived inside myth, settled there, a Headless Man whose single desire was to turn his own existence into a wondrous tale.

BABEL WITH LITTLE NATHALIE IN 1932

Chapter Two

THE HEADLESS MAN, PART II

1.

NOTHER STORYTELLER, Jorge Luis Borges, whose habit of telling stories was as bewildering as Isaac Babel's, once said: "Through the years, a man peoples a space with images of provinces, kingdoms, mountains, bays, ships, islands, fishes, rooms, tools, stars, horses, and people. Shortly before his death, he discovers that the patient labyrinth of lines traces the image of his own face."

And that's why Babel is so hard to imitate. He must have already been a writer at five or six, or at least recognized that words had their own powerful play. He would soon become a mind traveler, as merciless as myth, sucking in whatever happened to him. But right up to the Revolution this Headless Man had no real language of his own. Just as his juvenilia must have been pastiches of Maupassant, his first stories were pastiches of Gorky,

Gogol, and Chekhov. "Mama, Rima, and Alla," which Gorky published in *Letopis,* takes place in a Moscow that Babel knew little about. It features a martyred landlady and her two daughters, and seems to be told in several different voices, none of which belongs to Babel.

But it hardly matters, since Babel will later sanctify his first visit to *Letopis* in a second autobiographical fragment. "I went to see [Gorky] on Bolshaya Monetnaya Street. My heart kept pounding, then stopping dead."

Gorky agrees to read Babel's stories, and the Headless Man comes back in three days. "There are small nails [. . .] and there are nails as large as a finger," Gorky says, bringing a "long, powerful, delicately chiseled finger" up to Babel's eyes. "A writer's path, dear dreamer [. . .] is strewn with nails, mostly of the larger sort. You will have to walk upon them barefoot and they'll make you bleed. And with each year the blood will flow more freely."

And so the Headless Man walked on nails for Maxim Gorky. But nothing happened. And though he would insist upon the image of Gorky as his ultimate master, the bard and barefoot boy of Nizhni Novgorod had very little to teach him. Gorky's own rude style was good for Maxim Gorky, but his writing was humorless and without a single mask. Babel had a better teacher— himself.

It's 1920. He's living in Odessa with his bride and serving in the Gubkon (Provisional Party Committee). Sergei Ingulov, secretary of the Party Committee, enlists him as a war correspondent with the news service that would later turn into TASS. To blunt his Jewishness, Babel conspires with Ingulov to "wear" a Russian name, Kiril Vassilevich Lyutov. It's under this pseudonym that Babel is assigned to the Sixth Division of General Budenny's First Cavalry, with its Cossack warriors, as a writer for *Krasny Kavalerist* ("Red Cavalryman"), "our merciless newspaper [. . .], which every fighting man in the front lines wants to read, and after that with heroic spirit he hews down the Poles" ("A Letter").

Hiding within his Russian mask, he writes about Polish atrocities that have to be avenged by the Kavalerists. "Beat them, Red Fighters, clobber them to death, if it is the last thing you do! Right away! This minute! Now!" ("The Knights of Civilization").

In "Murderers Who Have Yet to Be Clubbed to Death," he tells us of the renegade Cossack captain Yakovlev, who sells himself to the Poles and pillages one little town after the other, leaving behind the corpses of "commissars, Yids, and Red Army soldiers [. . .] The horror of the Middle Ages pales in comparison to the bestiality of the Yakovlev bandits."

Lyutov is like a cut-rate Homer who loves to harangue. The horrors he describes don't even have the resonance of a good battle report. Kiril is a propagandist, put there to demonize the enemy. His sentences are overloaded, crowded with detail, and there isn't the least bit of space where the reader can dream on his own. But Kavalerists aren't meant to imagine. And Kiril embellishes every detail.

I don't blame Babel. He's writing for a military paper and has to fire up the troops, get them to fight. He has to dwarf his own sensibilities, *become* K. Lyutov, who rides on the propaganda train like a privileged character when he isn't out in the field taking notes as he bumps along on his nag, or has his own *tachanka*—"a buggy with a machine gun mounted on its back."

But there were two Babels riding on that *tachanka,* in the saddle, or on the propaganda train—one was that man bearing the documents of Kiril Lyutov, member of a mythic army on horseback that was prepared to free Poland from its Christ-loving, feudal oppressors as the first campaign to "export" Communism, and the other was a secretive writer keeping a diary in which he could shed the mask of Kiril. Nathalie Babel says that her father's persona, so elusive in his fiction, "is very clear" in the diary. But I'm not convinced. She claims that Babel, who'd never been on a horse, rode fifty miles on his first day with the Kavalerists, and that he scribbled the diary from the vantage point of his saddle. But the diary was as fictive as anything Babel wrote, whether he composed it on the back of a horse or not; it was, in fact, Babel's real beginning as a writer, the discovery of a voice that was for the first time *Babelesque*—with leaps of syntax, lyrical disconnections, as if he were tearing at language itself with a machine gun mounted on a murderous yet playful *tachanka* that could swallow up whole paragraphs and spit back sentences with missing pieces that cohered into a new design. It was no simple baptism under fire, with Babel studying the cruelty of war and catching the colors of war; rather, it was the diary of a writer forced to live in the present tense and finding his own savage shorthand that could seize the moment, render its maddening simultaneity, the ugliness and beauty that whirled in front of his eyes.

Babel's telegraphic style didn't come from the expediency of a man with saddle sores, who was writing on the run. It was the imaginative stop-and-go of someone who was learning to see in another way, where feelings had to be locked into the images that were spinning in his head. The little cavalryman from Odessa found himself with a split in his psyche—editorializing, gathering clichés aboard the propaganda train as Kiril Lyutov, and this same Kiril, who had to hide his Jewish identity from his Cossack "cousins" on the train and in the field, learning to tuck the almost melodic slaughter of Cossacks, Jews, and Poles into his own private landscape with a concise, brutal poetry, as he wore his Kavalerist uniform among the starving Jews of the shtetl, played at being Kiril when he didn't really have to play. . . .

The first entry, from June 3, 1920 (fifty-four pages are missing), finds Lyutov on the propaganda train, with its printing press and radio station sitting right near the front lines, so that the Red troopers can have a constant dose of ideology. And this is how Babel describes his fellow reporters on *Krasny Kavalerist:* "Lanky Zhukov, voracious Topolnik, the whole editorial crew unbelievably dirty people."

There was little comfort on the train. "Bad tea in borrowed mess cans." He enters the train's kitchen and strings together a series of nouns that will become the signature of his diary, the naming of things that have their own finality and force—"kasha, noon, sweat." The future author of *Red Cavalry* scribbles a note to himself: "describe the soldiers and women, fat, fed, sleepy."

Riding with Cossacks, he tells us in his shorthand: "Jewish pogrom, cut off beards, they [the Poles] always do. . . ."

At Zhitomir, in the Ukraine: "Night on the boulevard. The hunt for women." Babel becomes one more predator in the middle of this curious Cossack crusade. "Stars, night over the shtetl. A tall Cossack with an earring and a cap with a white top." He haunts the shtetl, repelled by the poverty, the forlorn faces, the smell of excrement, yet drawn to these Ukrainian Jews, so unlike the round and jolly worshipers at the Brodsky Synagogue in Odessa. "Discussion with Jews, my people, they think I'm Russian. . . ."

His truck breaks down during the journey to another town. "Cherries, I sleep, sweat in the sun." A medical assistant becomes the local celebrity: "In exchange for treatment women offered him their services, roasted chicken, and themselves."

He's billeted with a Jewish family, the Khasts, becomes a spy in their house, as "they think I don't understand Yiddish." He's a tin Cossack, one more hollow man. "I drink tea incessantly and sweat like a beast."

He's been promised his own *tachanka*. He borrows a horse and goes riding. "The sturdy huts glitter in the sun, roof tiles, iron, stones, apples, the stone schoolhouse"—objects dance around him with their own lyric pull, as if he's about to rediscover the world. And he offers the multiplicity of a universe in the shards of a sentence: "A Pole was caught in the rye, they hunted him down like an animal, wide fields, scarlet sun, golden fog, swaying grain . . ."

Rather than describe the destruction of an entire town, he focuses on a single victim: "Next to one of the huts lies a slaughtered cow that has only recently calved. Her bluish teats lying on the ground, just skin. An indescribable pity! A murdered young mother."

He's struck again and again by the Cossacks' grace and allure: "Describe their horses' garb, sabers in red velvet, curved sabers, vests, carpets over their saddles. Dressed poorly, though each of them has ten service jackets—it's doubtless a matter of chic."

Odessa is the underlying backdrop to so much of what he sees as he rides deeper into the Pale: "These Jews are like paintings: lanky, silent, long-bearded, not like ours, fat and jovial."

The carnage begins to crazy him, fill him with longings and desires: "Two girls are playing in the water, a strange, almost irrepressible urge to talk dirty, rough, slippery words."

But these "rough, slippery words" will also excite his own writing, empower him like a magician who can *control* the landscape, reorder it. Here he's describing a rape like some perverse idyll with which he can mask the pain. A Cossack "throws himself" on the Jewish bride of a one-eyed man's son "while their cart is being requisitioned, an incredible bout of cursing, the soldiers are eating meat out of pots, she, I will scream, her face, he pushes her against the wall . . ."

Whatever his flights of fancy, with his uniform and his sword, Babel realizes that he has no place among "the Cossacks, the marauding, the vanguard's vanguard. I don't belong." Yet he will make himself belong. Language will wed him to the carpets the Cossacks wear on their saddles; language will bring him closer to their lust: "Late night, red flag, silence, Red Army fighters thirsting for women."

Language will reveal the incongruity of everything, the sad wonder of what he was able to see: "I'm staying in a poor hut where a son with a big head plays the violin."

He has a sense of the Apocalypse, like some biblical prophet: "All our fighters: velvet caps, rapes, Cossack forelocks, battle, Revolution, and syphilis. The whole of Galicia is infected."

But he can move from the vast to the minuscule in the blink of an eye, point to the deliverance of a man on a horse. "We fly up the high road to Brody, I rock and sleep." And he can limit or enlarge a whole country, define Poland as "glittering garments draped over a decrepit body."

His technique is close to Eisen's montage: clashing images that multiply and manufacture stories: "I'm an outsider, in long trousers, not one of them, I am lonely, we ride on. . . ."

The shtetl, with its mystery and stink, disturbs him as much as any battle. He scuttles into a synagogue. "I pray, bare walls, some soldier or other is swiping the electric light bulbs."

2.

EVEN AS HE bares himself, it's hard to figure Babel out. We begin to realize that "Lyutov" isn't only a mask. Babel *is* Lyutov sometimes, even in the privacy of his scribbles. And it's this curious jumping from persona to persona that makes the diary so evocative and difficult to pin down.

As usual, his *Avtobiographiya* is all wrong. It wasn't in 1923 that he taught himself to write. It was during the months when he had his own *tachanka* and a piebald horse and a seat on the propaganda train, where he not only kept his diary but also prepared sketches for the memoir or tales he intended to write. The sketches are much more mannered, artful, and schematic, the writer looking into his own writerly mirror. "A poem in prose" is one of his headings. "We gallop off—I keep throwing books away—a piece of my soul."

That kind of preciousness doesn't enter the diary, where Babel surprises us as much as he surprises himself. The shtetl is a more powerful obsession *and* motif than the Cossacks themselves. "I roam about the shtetl, there is pitiful, powerful, undying life inside the Jewish hovels, young ladies in white stockings, long coats, so few fat people."

—so few fat people.

The images haunt him and haunt us. Babel's ride into the Pale with the Red Cavalry must have dislodged his many masks, educated him more than any summons from Maxim Gorky to go into the world—the shtetl was the closing off of the world, a psychic and cultural imprisonment, a terrible laceration as these hovel dwellers were caught between the Cossacks and the Poles. And Babel couldn't escape them, not even in his Cossack guise, with a sword clattering between his legs. And it is this lament that informs the diary, the strange religious power of the Pale—young ladies in white stockings—that will mark Babel, make him much, much more than a Headless Man.

Chapter Three

KIRIL LYUTOV

1.

Iᴛ's 2055. We're in Washington, D.C. I can recognize most of the monuments, but something is amiss: cars don't move across horizontal highways anymore; they dart along gravitational grids, while choppers that look like giant eraser wheels can land anywhere on a dime. It's practically a perfect world, at least on the outside. The homicide rate has gone down to zero, thanks to the Department of Precrime in D.C. Murders that might have happened in the immediate future can be previsualized by the "Precogs," oracles who live in a huge round tub called the Temple. There are three of them, male twins, Dash (for Dashiell) and Arthur (for Arthur Conan Doyle), and their "sister," Agatha (for Agatha Christie, of course), who's much brighter than the twins and is a kind of super sibyl. Their memory streams—the images they produce in their swollen heads—

can be interpreted by detectives, who then ride on their eraser wheels to the precrime scene and catch the "culprit." But something happens to John Anderton (Tom Cruise), chief of the precrime squad. The oracles name him as the next murderer-to-be. Realizing that he's been set up, Anderton steals the sibyl from her tub, and tries to unravel the reason for his own preselection. Thus you have the essentials of Steven Spielberg's *Minority Report* (2002), a futuristic film noir that feels frighteningly close to certain premises about crime in the twenty-first century. "We're more like clergy than cops," say the members of Anderton's squad.

But it's Agatha who interests me most. Played by Samantha Morton with the eerie charm of an actual sibyl, she curls up in Anderton's car and asks, "Is it now?"

John doesn't get her, and neither do we. "Is it now?" Agatha asks again. And we begin to realize her dilemma. Bottled up in her tub, with her brain navigating like mad into the near future, she's lost the present tense.

"I'm tired, tired of the future," she tells John. And we grasp the horror of Agatha's earlier line.

Is it now?

All our lives we've taken the present for granted, as if it belonged to us, as if it flowed out of the past with our individual copyright, and suddenly Agatha forces us to confront the fact that *now* has its own memory stream, that it doesn't belong to us at all, that it's a multiplicity of "hits" we love to privatize into our own little saga of ourselves. Perhaps this saga keeps us sane.

But *Red Cavalry* (*Konarmiya*), Babel's fictional portrait of his time with the Cossacks, is the closest thing we have to Agatha's ordeal. It reproduces the present tense with all its simultaneity and shocks, and shows us the disconnection not only of "battle," but of our very lives, and of our terrible, terrible need to narratize, to form lines of attack when there are none. The originality of *Konarmiya* is that it is a text in search of a narrator. This never would have happened if Babel hadn't experienced the Polish campaign in a very particular way. He's a writer from Odessa pretending to be a Russian war correspondent, Kiril Lyutov. Kiril makes up his history as he goes along: he has a law degree from St. Petersburg University, a Jewish mother, and a wife who's left him (Babel did study "law" for a little while in Petersburg, did have a Jewish mother, and a wife who "left" him to go to Paris). The Cossacks call Kiril "Four-Eyes," and though they have contempt for him as an intellectual and a city boy who's never been on a horse, he does become their scribe. Peacocks who are proud of their *chub* (the forelock that accompanies their otherwise shaven skull), they have a distinctive, spicy speech, decorated with their own private grammar, but they're also peasants who can neither read nor write, and it's "Four-Eyes" who has to transcribe their melodic voice into words on a page; it's "Four-Eyes" who has to read *Pravda* and *Krasny Kavalerist* (their own paper) to them. And this Lyutov is hardly at a disadvantage; language is as much a weapon as their curved Circassian sabers; he can censor them whenever he wishes, distort their own speech, dilute their power. He wears a cavalryman's uniform, and he's his own kind of Cossack when he parades among impoverished Jews in the Pale of Settlement. Much of

Babel's diary is taken up with this pretense and with his wants. He can be as cruel as any Cossack when he snatches a bun out of a child's fist, and shares some of the Cossacks' legendary lust. "I am sad because there's no one to copulate with." He can be a war correspondent *and* a diarist, babble in different tongues. But something happens in the stories. Babel's persona won't stay put. Voices run all over the place, as if he were his very own sibyl, trying to capture the present tense of war.

Critics like to see Lyutov as the unifying narrator of *Red Cavalry*. I do not. Lyutov's the fiction of a fiction, a sort of illness that drags across *Red Cavalry*, like the horse that drags Lyutov by the foot; we might even say the entire narrative could be that of a man being dragged by a horse while he's dreaming.

The narrator is unnamed for most of the book. And when he's finally called Lyutov, in the twenty-fifth tale, it doesn't mean much. Lyutov could be anybody—a shadow from hell, a soldier, or someone playing a soldier. The narrator also assumes other voices, as he transcribes the letters that certain Cossacks dictate to him in their own "voice," but they have no voice other than the one Lyutov allows them. There's a name for this in Russian—*skaz:* the colloquial speech of a storyteller who is less educated than the reader or the person to whom he's telling the story. Mark Twain used his own kind of *skaz* in *Huckleberry Finn.* But if Mark Twain is Huck's "scribe," we never feel that he's inserting himself between Huck and the reader, or limiting Huck's voice. As the author, he may navigate Huck down the Mississippi, but he doesn't interfere. We never feel removed from Huck's own "moral passion," or from the *roundness* of his voice. But with

Babel there are at least three or four degrees of separation—the looseness of transcribing from one voice to another, the secretiveness of the narrator's own voice, and the moments when the narrator splits into several personas and Babel can no longer tell the difference between Lyutov and himself, and we can no longer believe in the narration, as if the stories themselves were having a breakdown. . . .

2.

RED CAVALRY OPENS with "Crossing into Poland," when the "blackened Zbruch" twists into foamy knots and Babel and his fellow cavalrymen wade across the river. The narrator has just gone through battle and he imagines the world around him in metaphors of mutilation. "The orange sun rolled down the sky like a lopped-off head." And he can't break away from "the smell of yesterday's blood, of slaughtered horses." We hop from image to image, from the yellowing rye to buckwheat rising like a wall to the serpentine trails of the moon, as if past, present, and future merge into "the square black patches of the wagons," with the sound of whistling and singing right beside us: we already feel a kind of vertigo, and we haven't gotten beyond the second paragraph.

"The special effect of [Babel's] work is of being placed outside time, of being caught in a single recurring event, of going from innocence to knowledge in a flash," and of being like an amnesiac who cannot find his moorings. Babel's work unsettles us, and is made to unsettle, because it does not offer us the usual lifeline of a beginning, a middle, and an end. We plunge into the narrative, and either we swim or disappear into "the noisy torrent."

The narrator reaches Novograd and is billeted in the house of a pregnant woman, two red-haired Jewish men, and a third man who is asleep, huddled against the wall. All we can find is filth—human excrement, pieces of fur coats, fragments of crockery left over from some lost seder.

Clearly disgusted, he orders the woman to clean up the debris. "What a filthy way to live!" The pair of redheads jump around "like Japs in a circus act," clean up, and produce a feather bed "that has been disemboweled." The narrator lies down near the wall, next to the third man. He starts to dream about Savitsky, the commander of the Sixth Division, who is chasing the brigade commander and shoots him twice between the eyes; with his head torn open, both of the brigade commander's eyes fall to the ground. Savitsky shouts at him, and he could have been shouting at the narrator, whose hysterical need to name things, to blanket the world with images, seems to cover up fears about his own manhood—if his eyes fall out, he will lose this power to name and will be exposed as a fraud. His eyes are akin to his sexuality; he arouses himself with words—he cannot name if he cannot see—and also soothes himself, resting like "a majestic moon."

The pregnant woman drags him out of his dream. He's been tossing in his sleep, she tells him, and pushing her father about. She uncovers her father, who is dead. His throat has been torn out "and his face cleft in two." And the narrator, again covering his emotion and fear, is quick to notice the *design* of the dead man, his blue beard "clotted like a lump of lead."

The Jewess tells her father's tale. *Pan,* she says, the Poles cut his throat while he begged them to kill him in the yard so that his daughter couldn't see him die. But the Poles still cut his throat in front of her. And now the woman cries into the narrator's face with a sudden violence: "I should wish to know where in the whole world you could find another father like my father?"

And we've moved from one eternity to another in three pages: from the pomp of a victorious army crossing into another country to the terrifying dignity of an old man to the cry of his daughter—a cry much more legitimate than the claims of any war.

The narrator is left with nothing, and so are we: we've entered a landscape where we can find lots of ornament but little comfort, where the language finally eats at us, mocks us, and like drugged men and women, we're never quite sure who we are or where we are. . . .

And now we're introduced to our first lesson in *skaz,* as the narrator offers us a letter that has been dictated to him by Vasily Kurdyukov, a Cossack lad in "our special group" ("The Letter"). He assures us that he hasn't changed a word and then tells us about the scraps of material that he's left out.

Vasily is writing to his mother. He belongs to the Political Section, to the cavalry's newspaper. He talks about his father, who served with the Whites and killed one of his sons (also a Kavalerist). He'd been a cop under the old regime. And as the

Reds began to win, Vasily's father "dyed his beard shamelessly from red to black." It's the first of many disguises that crop up again and again in *Red Cavalry*. But the ultimate *disguiser* is Lyutov himself. He saunters into battle with an unloaded gun; in fact, his gun is never loaded as he moves from tale to tale on his *tachanka* or his horse. Dolgushov, a telephonist, is sitting by a road. "His belly had been torn out. The entrails hung over his knees, and the heartbeats were visible" ("The Death of Dolgushov"). He doesn't want to be tortured by the Poles. He asks Lyutov to finish him off. Lyutov refuses and rides away. It's Alfonka, the platoon commander, who shoots the telephonist in the mouth. And he's prepared to kill Lyutov, too. "You guys in specs have about as much pity for chaps like us as a cat for a mouse."

Alfonka's indictment cuts to the bone. The narrator is toying with the Cossacks, slumming in his own way. In "My First Goose," the Cossacks reject him until he kills a goose and obliges his landlady to cook it for him. This little act pleases them, and they welcome him into their company. There's something staged about the whole performance, and Babel offers us a clue when he has the narrator declare: "Already the moon hung above the yard like a cheap earring."

The narrator falls asleep with his five new Cossack friends in a hayloft, "our legs intertwined. I dreamed: and in my dreams saw women. But my heart, stained with bloodshed, grated and brimmed over."

And why don't I believe him? His lament seems out of proportion to the deed. The more eloquent the narrator becomes the more dishonest he is. Killing the goose is a trifle compared to *not* killing Dolgushov.

In the next story, "The Rabbi," we catch one of our few naked glimpses of the narrator. He shucks off his mask, declares himself a Jew from Odessa to the grand rabbi of Zhitomir, the last of a great dynasty.

"What is the Jew's occupation?" asks the rabbi in his own mock inquisition.

"I am putting into verse the adventures of Hersch of Ostropol."

This was Babel's own line of work. In 1918 he'd published a story about Hersch, a trickster and schlemiel from Yiddish folklore. And in the Cossack tales, Babel-Lyutov is often a trickster, a schlemiel on a horse who has to plunk his revolver on the kitchen table if he wants his Jewish landlady to feed him. And when Akinfiev, a syphilitic Cossack in "After the Battle," exposes him as a cavalryman without a single cartridge, he fights with the Cossack. Akinfiev falls down and starts to bleed. Lyutov grows eloquent again. "Evening flew up to the sky like a flock of birds," he says, "and darkness crowned me with its watery wreath," as if Lyutov were some little suffering Christ who implores fate "to grant me the simplest of proficiencies—the ability to kill my fellow-men." And we're supposed to sympathize with his *humaneness,* support the Babelesque irony behind it—a soldier who can't kill—and forget the toy soldier who's prepared to set fire to his landlady's house if she won't feed him.

But the narrator loses his eloquence after the most brutal moment in the book ("Berestechko"). Some Cossacks are about to

shoot an old Jew with a silver beard for spying. The old man strug-
gles and begins to scream. A machine-gunner named Kudrya
grabs him by the head and tucks it under his arm. "The Jew
stopped screaming [. . .] Kudrya drew out his dagger with his
right hand and carefully, without splashing himself, cut the old
man's throat."

There are no epic images here, just a description of murder,
simple and direct, without the blanket of metaphor, but if we
shut our eyes we might have a vision of the same peasant-soldier
slaughtering some lamb, "without splashing himself."

Babel's silence is much more disturbing than any comment
Lyutov might care to make. But other readers of *Red Cavalry*
don't agree. Richard Hallett talks of the book's "basic heartlessness." And Frank O'Connor, himself a master of the short story,
can't decide whether he should regard Babel "as a real writer or
a dangerous lunatic."

Patricia Carden is a much keener critic. We resist *Red Cavalry,* feel that we've "been dealt a blow with a powerful instrument," forcing us into the dream of a narrative that has no
connective tissue. The stories are like melodic episodes that
leave us utterly stranded and alone. Babel is recapturing his own
dislocation, when narrators have nowhere to go. . . .

In "Berestechko," the narrator speaks the only way he can.
After the murder of the old Jew, he has to distance himself from
the ghetto in order to preserve his sanity and stay alive. He kills
the entire ghetto with his own kind of cartridges—words.
Berestechko begins to stink: "a violent smell of rotten herrings
emanates from all its inhabitants [. . .] and instead of human

beings there go about mere faded schemata of frontier misfortunes."

But this isn't enough. He has to blind himself, or at least discover an image of blindness. He climbs out of the ghetto and into the "sacked castle" of the counts who once presided over Berestechko. "I wandered past walls where nymphs with gouged-out eyes were leading a choral dance."

And perhaps we've stumbled upon some sort of key: terror rules the stories, a blinding terror, and the narrator has to sing and dance like Hersch, play the fool, if he's going to survive all that he sees. His manuscripts, locked in a trunk, can't help him here—nothing can, except his own music.

Frank O'Connor compares Babel to Hemingway, says both have one thing in common: "a romanticism of violence." O'Connor is wrong again. The nearest analogue we have to *Red Cavalry* is Hemingway's *In Our Time,* but it's not "a romanticism of violence" that holds the books together—it's the dreamlike distortion of war. Both Lyutov and Nick Adams (Hemingway's fictional mask) wander across the landscape like drugged men. But Nick is reliable, and Nick is no Hersch. He's not a trickster. Yet we feel the same dislocation in him and in Lyutov, the same sense of amnesia. Nick can't sleep. He was blown up during the war, and he's convinced that if he falls asleep, his soul will leap out of his body and never come back. And so he remembers the streams he'd fished as a boy, revisits them like some haunted angler and clutches at the details. Lyutov isn't like that. Lyutov dreams all the time. But in his sleep men lose their eyes. . . .

It's the nature of narrative that really links both authors and their early books. As Hemingway said to Ilya Ehrenburg in the midst of the Spanish Civil War, after he discovered Babel during an air raid in Madrid: "I have been criticized for writing too concisely, but I find that Babel's style is even more concise than mine." Both men were *hunters* who realized the merciless drama of where a sentence ended and began. "No iron can stab the heart with such force as a period put just at the right place," Babel says in "Guy de Maupassant." And he could have been Hemingway here. They were among the very first writers to insist that the reader had to be brought right into the narrative: fiction was like detective work that depended on the reader's own participation. The reader lived in those white islands between the words. But none of this might have happened if "Hem" and Babel hadn't gone to war—war would mark them with an ambiguity worse than any wound. Hem liked to brag that he'd served in the Arditi, the Italian shock troops of World War I who were as notorious as the Red Cavalry would become in the Russian Civil War. But Hem was only a boy in the Red Cross, an ambulance driver who switched to canteen service because he wanted to be near the front line. And he was blown up weeks before his nineteenth birthday, while distributing chocolate and cigarettes in the trenches; he would have pieces of shrapnel embedded in his buttocks for the rest of his life, remain with a little forest of scars on his legs. And Babel would return from Poland with a severe case of asthma and lice all over his body; a few of his friends had even given him up for dead. Hem would adopt the swagger of an air marshal, and Babel would often behave like a man who was still rocking along on a horse, but whatever their pretense and personal fables, they'd absorbed the no-man's-land of military conflict . . . and what that conflict could do on a page of prose.

Reading *Red Cavalry* and *In Our Time* is like looking at the world through barbed wire while the wire is moving out from under you. We catch the jarred edge of things, the rip and tear of memory. The language both men use—a savage shorthand—doesn't glamorize; it's about the closing off that comes from shock, little time bombs as crisp as articles of war. Hem may have delivered candy for the Red Cross, and Babel may have been Kiril Lyutov on his propaganda train, but they were still "combatants." A writer, Babel would say, was like "a soldier on reconnaissance."

Chapter Four

ARGAMAK

1.

C YNTHIA OZICK writes like a lost daughter of Isaac Babel—a picaro with her very own plumage. In her introduction to the master's complete works, she compares him with that ghostly internal wanderer and waif, Franz Kafka, who starved to death because he could no longer swallow. Kafka was, she says, "the man who thinks but barely lives," a metaphysician of sick souls who navigated entire worlds from his private closet. But Babel "lives, lives, lives! [. . .] He is a trickster, rapscallion, ironist, wayward lover, imprudent impostor." The list could go on and on. Babel himself loved to support that impression, to play the picaro. In *Red Cavalry*, he summons up Khlebnikov, commander of the 1st Squadron, who has lost his white stallion to Savitsky, his own divisional commander: Savitsky simply stole the horse, and Khlebnikov can't recover from the unfairness of it.

He resigns from the Party, writes a declaration—"I am, comrades, a lover of white horses"—and the Party can't give him back the horse. He's demobilized, drummed out of the service. And Lyutov sees in Khlebnikov some kind of brother. "We were both shaken by the same passions. Both of us looked at the world as a meadow in May—a meadow traversed by women and horses" ("The Story of a Horse").

We're supposed to read this as the *real* Babel, the man who preferred meadows in May, with a swath of women and horses. Horses are as powerful a motif in *Red Cavalry* as the Cossacks themselves. Afonka Bida, a platoon commander, has his horse shot right out from under him. "Farewell, Stepan," he says to the dying animal, bowing from the waist "like a woman seized with hysterics in church."

He abandons his own unit and starts punishing Poles.

"A horse is like a father," says one of the men in Bida's platoon, "saves one's life time and again. Bida will be lost without his horse."

And he is. The whole countryside bears the traces of Bida's butchering.

"He's hunting around for a horse," the platoon sings about its commander.

Two weeks go by as Bida sets fire to village after village in his "despairing, lone-wolf attacks."

Lyutov's division takes a particular town. The men believe that Bida has had his head bashed in by Galician peasants in the woods. But suddenly he rides up to them on a tall gray stallion, without his left eye. He's glad to give his eye if it means capturing a magnificent horse.

His men look at him in wonder, pull on the stallion's tail, count its teeth. They're envious. They'd all give up an eye to have such a horse . . . ("Afonka Bida").

Red Cavalry doesn't end with a horse or a horseman, but with a prince who has lost his pants. Elijah, a rabbi's son *and* a dying revolutionary, is laid out on board the propaganda train, with his maddening mix of Lenin and Maimonides—he's a Jewish poet and propagandist, like Babel himself, but at least Elijah has actual cartridges with his pages from Solomon's Song of Songs. And Lyutov finishes off the story with another one of his lies. "And I, who can scarce contain the tempests of my imagination within this age-old body of mine, I was there beside my brother when he breathed his last" ("The Rabbi's Son").

Lyutov wasn't there at all. He was drifting in his own mirage of words. But *we* can't forget that curious dilemma of a rabbi's son who found his own new faith in the Revolution, and dies with his poetry and phylacteries. And Babel? He's Elijah's double who didn't die, who has to go deeper into the whirlwind. . . .

And then, six years after the book appeared, Babel wrote a new ending, called it "Argamak: An Unpublished Chapter of the *Red Cavalry*." Ever since his first success in Moscow, Babel had also become a lover of white stallions, a writer who lived on a stud farm, who mingled with jockeys like the ex-cavalryman he'd never been.

"Argamak" is his own story of a horse.

"I resolved to transfer to the active forces," Lyutov says in the opening line. There are no horses, but Lyutov is given a horse. His squadron commander punishes a Cossack who has killed a couple of captured officers, deprives him of Argamak. But Lyutov can't really handle the horse. "I would wobble like a sack on the stallion's long lean spine."

Argamak's hind legs swell up. He grows thin. His old master appears, dressed in galoshes and rags. "Argamak stretched out his long neck and neighed toward his master, neighed in a soft squeal, like a horse in the desert."

Lyutov transfers to another squadron, where he's triumphant on a lesser horse, having learned the Cossack style of riding from Argamak. He's accepted as a cavalryman, but it's at a terrible price. Babel's own dream has intruded upon the narrative. Still, it doesn't spoil *Red Cavalry*.

We tolerate "Argamak" as another bouncing mirror in a text that metamorphoses in front of our eyes. The genius of the book is that it behaves like a cannibal that can swallow its own parts and spit them back at us in a new configuration. . . .

Babel was never a horseman no matter how hard he tried. It was the pose of a picaro. The craftsman who didn't like to talk about books. But when he was with Olesha, his only rival as a fiction writer, *he* was the hunger artist who longed not to be alone. Olesha grew even more silent than Babel under Stalin's thumb, and drank too much. "Don't overdo it, Yura," Babel would sigh in his company, "[or] I'll have no one to talk with."

2.

IT WASN'T BLIND luck that brought Babel to the Kavalerists in the spring of 1920. His family considered it a suicidal act—a Yid from Odessa riding with Cossacks who were a pogrom unto themselves, the tsar's most loyal ally in killing Jews and putting down rebellion. But Babel's encounter with the Cossacks would crystallize him in a way that no mythical meeting with Gorky ever could.

He'd become a soldier of sorts, even with his empty gun. He had his own ambulance *tachanka* and other duties that propelled him into the arms of the general staff. He was some kind of military historian, attached to his division as its very own "scribe," writing battle reports, interrogating prisoners; during battle he would climb aboard his ambulance and help with the wounded. Babel was *everywhere*. Suicidal or not, he'd picked the right campaign and had positioned himself within it as the propagandist who held a whole bunch of keys: he could observe and participate, blend into the battle or remain apart, while experimenting with his fictional personas, and "like the classic picaro," wearing his own false identity, Babel "found himself a character in a wholly different picaresque," where nothing was what it seemed—devils were invoked and blood was spilled out of misconceived malice.

The Polish peasants thought that all Jews were Bolsheviks; therefore they had the right to kill as many as they could. And the Jews of the Pale were startled to learn that the Bolsheviks who had come to liberate them were only Cossacks like other Cossacks, ready to steal and rape. And Babel, as some phantasmagoric information officer, would feed them fairy tales about the wonders of the Revolution, fairy tales that he half believed. Hadn't Babel arrived with a crusading army? *These* crusaders cared about no one but themselves. They were marauders with a Red star. . . .

Did Babel realize that he would touch upon an historical moment when he volunteered to join the Cossack crusade? We have no record of him as a Chekist or as a foot soldier on the Rumanian front. These were mosaics for his *Avtobiographiya*, put there to build the aura of an Odessa bookworm who transforms himself into a Soviet hero. He would write "The Road" (published in 1932, the same year as "Argamak"), about his adventures as a picaro in Petersburg during the Civil War. Our narrator leaves "the crumbling front," arrives in Kiev, gets on the train to Petersburg with a Jewish teacher and his wife. But a telegrapher climbs aboard, looks at the teacher's travel permit, and shoots him in the face. Then a hunchbacked muzhik slices off the teacher's sexual organs and stuffs them into the wife's mouth, telling her that now she can eat something kosher.

Next, all Jews are thrown off the train. The hunchback strips off the narrator's boots and coat, steals the four gold coins that his mother had sewn into his underwear, hits him on the back of the neck, and cackles in Yiddish, "Run away, Chaim."

And he runs, his bare feet sinking into snow. He arrives in a shtetl and informs us with his usual élan: "There was no doctor at the hospital to amputate my frostbitten feet." The Soviets move him out on a cart in the middle of the night. His feet heal. He arrives in Petersburg by train, sleeping beneath the muzzle of a howitzer.

He can't enter into the city's secrets. "This frozen, basalt Venice stood transfixed." He stops at the Cheka headquarters on Gorokhovaya Street, shows the commandant a letter from Vanya Kalugin, a sergeant in his old regiment who is now with the Cheka. The commandant tells him to find Kalugin at the Anichkov Palace.

Our narrator trudges across Petersburg. "The Nevsky Prospekt flowed into the distance like the Milky Way. Dead horses lay along it like milestones. Their legs, pointing upward, supported the descending sky."

He finds Kalugin sitting in the palace next to a table with a heap of toys. He falls asleep on the table, shoving the toys aside. He wakes up on a sofa. "The lights of a chandelier danced above me in a waterfall of glass."

Kalugin carries him like a baby into a bathtub, gives the barefoot boy a bath, pouring water over him with a bucket. Our narrator gets into a robe with buckles, tailored for a giant—it's the robe of Tsar Alexander III, who weighed 325 pounds and once lived in the palace.

They drink tea together as "stars [stream] over the crystal walls of our glasses." They smoke cigars thick as a finger— Alexander's own cigars, the gift of a sultan. And our narrator looks at the giant's robe, which has been mended many times. The toys on the table once belonged to Alexander's son, Nicholas II, the last of the tsars, murdered with his family at Ekaterinburg in 1918, the same year that our narrator and Kalugin pass a whole night playing with his toys.

In the morning Kalugin takes him to Gorokhovaya Street. "He's one of us," Kalugin explains to the chairman of the Petersburg Cheka. "His father is a storekeeper, a merchant, but he's washed his hands of them. . . . He knows languages."

He's given a military uniform and food coupons, and in a corner of the City Hall he starts translating the "depositions of diplomats, agents provocateurs, and spies."

And in a single day our narrator has everything: "clothes, food, work, and comrades true in friendship and death . . . That is how, thirteen years ago, a wonderful life filled with thought and joy began for me."

The story is as ambiguous and rich in coloration as anything Babel ever wrote. But the tag he places at the end reads like a kiss to Comrade Stalin and the Central Committee, as if Babel were preparing his own progress report as a Bolshevik pilgrim. Stalin has demanded a prose that serves the Party. And "The Road" is Babel's little wayward dance toward the perimeters of Bolshevik reality. Babel now identifies himself as a Chekist and a good soldier. It's one more fairy tale, but it's marked with hysteria. The hunchback who stuffs the sexual organs of the Jewish teacher into his wife's mouth is like an ogre who's come out of a magic forest. And Petersburg, with its fields of ice and dead horses holding up the sky, is like an enchanted town that lives within the walls of its own enchanted clock. . . .

Babel must have been dreaming about the Anichkov Palace for a long time. He told Paustovsky in 1921 of his "unofficial residence" at the palace, how he'd slept on Tsar Alexander's divan and smoked "fat, pink cigarettes" instead of cigars, cigarettes from the Sultan of Turkey.

Yet nothing he told Paustovsky was quite as fantastic or disturbingly factual as his summer with the Red Cavalry. How could Babel have known that the Polish campaign would be the last significant mounting of cavalry in modern European warfare? The Red Cavalry, with its "16,000 active sabers," would soon disappear. Babel himself marks its death cry when he has a full squadron of Kavalerists ride into the woods to avoid four enemy bombers, while their wounded commander attacks the plane with a certain panache and is cut to pieces.

The Red Cavalry had been the Revolution's most successful and celebrated cadre. It was created in November 1919 to counter those Cossacks who had sided with the Whites. The Kavalerists would become an instantaneous myth—the entire cavalry had been given over to the Cossacks. They were irresistible as they charged with their red banners shivering in the sky. Stalin himself was their "leader," since he was the political commissar of the southern front. Red Cavalry commanders remained among his favorites, and weren't touched when Stalin decided to plow into his own generals during the Great Purge. But within ten years of the disastrous Polish campaign, the Cossacks themselves would be persecuted. Not even the Boss could mold them into shock troops.

There was that little moment when a man in a mask appeared on the propaganda train, writing for a Cossack newspaper that the Cossacks couldn't read, riding into a Poland that had been carved up by two or three different empires, and encountering an enigmatic world of poor Jews, since the path of the Polish campaign was the Pale of Settlement itself. And Babel, the Revolution's own writer, was troubled and half crazed by what he saw—marauding and rape by both sides, the Reds and the Catholic Poles. Whatever we might call it, he suffered a breakdown. He would return to Odessa at the end of the year with glazed eyes, months after the Red Cavalry had been sent into reserve. Later, in a story that wasn't published together with *Red Cavalry,* he would write about his experiences with the cruel tone of a cavalier. Six Ukrainian anarchists have raped a Jewish maid. And when Lyutov hears about it he "decide[s] to find out what a woman looks like after being raped six times" ("Makhno's Boys"). The cruelty continues as Lyutov describes how she walks "with the heavy gait of a cavalryman whose numb legs have just touched the ground after a very long ride." But the centerpiece of the story is neither Lyutov nor the maid. It's Kikin, an errand boy for the anarchists who assisted in the rape—he held down the girl's arms—but couldn't seem to rape her himself. Disgruntled half the time, he's considered a simpleton who likes to walk about on his hands. But he's the only human barometer we have left; and Babel, like Kikin, is also someone who spent most of the campaign walking around on his hands. . . .

I suspect that his ride with the Kavalerists had broken his revolutionary zeal. He'd gone through the war in a kind of dream state, as a wounded picaro, where the boundaries between him and his masks began to merge; this sense of an hallucinated self would provide *Red Cavalry* with much of its power. But he kept to the role of the picaro. Perhaps it was the one means of escaping the absurdity of his situation. The Revolution wasn't interested in writers who walked on their hands. It wanted soldiers, not verbal acrobats. . . .

3.

RED CAVALRY IS one of those books, like Melville's *Confidence-Man* or Conrad's *Heart of Darkness* or Fitzgerald's *Gatsby*, that are larger, more mysterious, than our means of interpreting them. They grow more and more modern, seem to mirror the strangeness within and around us. Saul Bellow addressed this "affliction" of the modern when he wrote that "narrative art itself has dissolved." The sense of the single person, or narrating force, has skipped town. "Instead of a unitary character with his unitary personality, his ambitions, his passions, his soul, his fate, we find in modern literature an oddly dispersed, ragged, mingled, broken, amorphous creature whose outlines are everywhere, whose being is bathed in mind as the tissues are bathed in blood, and who is impossible to circumscribe in any scheme of time."

Kiril Lyutov.

Red Cavalry is filled with Kiril's own darker doubles. In "Two Ivans," Kiril's horse has been killed. He stops to take a leak. While buttoning up his pants, he feels "splashes of something" on his hand. He lights his little lantern and sees lying on the ground a Pole he had splattered with his piss. "It was pouring out of his mouth, bubbling between his teeth, gathered in his empty sockets." He finds a notebook near the corpse, with personal expenses, "a list of plays to be given at the Cracow theater, the date of the birthday of a woman called Marie-Louise"—a writer's notebook, random, with a fury of detail.

Lyutov plays with us again when he wipes the skull of his "unknown brother" with a page of Polish propaganda. "Night flew toward me on mettlesome horses," horses that disturb the soul. Babel may have been the poet of sunlight, but *Red Cavalry* collects images of a hellish night, where the moon is green as a lizard . . . or loiters in the sky like a beggar woman, and morning doesn't want to come, as it oozes over Lyutov "like chloroform on a hospital table."

He's one more prince of the night, pissed-upon, with eye sockets that reflect nothing, give nothing back, as spurious as that notebook on the ground, with its riddle of numbers and names, and words that leap out at us and Lyutov.

The Soviets could not bear to see this, a "hero" whose persona seems to unravel on every page. It took a French critic, Roland Barthes, to read Babel for us. "Style is indifferent to society," says Barthes in *Writing Degree Zero;* it is the writer's "glory and his prison, it is his solitude." Great writing is a kind of agraphia, "it is anti-communication, it is intimidating"—it longs to say that which cannot be said. "Modernism begins with the search for a literature which is no longer possible." It is like a text that explodes, that destroys itself, crawling deep into the night. Babel takes us into the belly of the beast and holds our hand. His book is about a terrifying, brutal loneliness, but we aren't lonely as we read it. He's captured that one perverse moment in the Revolution where the lawless dance of the Cossacks was outside ideology, was pure ritual, and their "mettlesome horses" belonged neither to the Russians nor the Poles, but to that long lament of language, the sadness of song.

Chapter Five

BENYA KRIK

1.

YEARS AGO I HAPPENED upon a photograph called *A Jewish Giant at Home with His Parents in the Bronx, N.Y.*, and immediately thought of Babel. The Jewish giant could have been one more gargoyle in Babel's portrait of Odessa. He has a special shoe on his left foot, a cane in his right hand, and he has to stoop in order not to bump the ceiling with his head. He's suffering from acromegaly, sometimes known as giantism (Goliath suffered from the same disease). Dated 1970, the photograph is by Diane Arbus.

Her giant has curly hair and a colossal jaw. He's smiling at his parents, who have a look of total befuddlement on their faces. They're tiny people, the two of them, seem half his size. The giant is sloppily dressed, but his father is impeccable in a dark jacket and horn-rimmed glasses; behind him is a lamp that tilts right out of the picture.

The photograph is deliberately unarranged, almost with a randomness of detail, but in that randomness Arbus has captured the parents' dilemma: Old World immigrants gazing at the son they've spawned, this monster of the New World—a Jewish giant.

"Freaks was a thing I photographed a lot," Arbus told a group of students at the Rhode Island School of Design shortly before she killed herself in 1971. "There's a quality of legend about freaks. Like a person in a fairy tale who stops you and demands that you answer a riddle. Most people go through life dreading they'll have a traumatic experience. Freaks were born with their trauma. They've already passed their test. They're aristocrats."

Of course, her Jewish giant wasn't born a giant. He didn't get his colossal jaw until adolescence. But his trauma is still as sad as a fairy tale.

"It's what I've never seen before that I recognize," Arbus once said, and we can imagine Babel coming to the same conclusion as he wandered through the debris of Poland and began to frame things like a photographer would, and seize whatever he saw with words.

Babel had Diane Arbus' inquisitiveness, that sense of familiarity with the unfamiliar, a desire to seek out what was strange or new . . . and translate it into a series of images that were like snapshots in continual motion. He would have adored the giant, felt right at home in his parents' Bronx apartment, he who could have

turned the entire planet into a fairy tale filled with gargoyles—
that's how his eye "sat" on things. Even Viktor Shklovsky, one of
Babel's best readers, oversimplified the dynamics of his art:
"Babel's Cossacks are all insufferably and ineffably handsome."
They're only handsome when Babel decides to *see* them as handsome. They can also be syphilitic and grim, like the platoon commander Afonka after he loses an eye—"a pink swelling gaped
repulsively in his charred face" ("Afonka Bida").

The Cossacks are monsters in a fairy tale of war.

The Red Cavalry was defeated in Poland, and the sick man
who returned to Odessa at the end of 1920 with lice all over him,
who'd already been reported dead, didn't start writing about
tachankas. His first published story after the Polish campaign
was about Benya Krik, and Benya had nothing to do with revolu-
tions. Babel had gone back to that period right after the pogrom,
into the mythical turf of his own childhood, to the Moldavanka
where he'd been born, and not to Nikolaev, where he could ice-
skate in his own yard and endure the pogrom like some perverse
hallucination.

Babel was running from Kiril Lyutov—Kiril could evaporate
in front of your eyes. Kiril wasn't safe. Babel went into the black-
ness of the Moldavanka and found his fairy tale.

2.

THE CRITIC AND translator Raymond Rosenthal calls Benya
Krik "a Jewish Cossack," says the stories about Benya "are based
to a large extent on fact. Odessa provided fertile material," as if it

were overrun with bandits from whom Babel could choose at will. But there was only one Benya Krik. He's as mysterious as Magwitch or Melville's Bartleby, those other great gargoyles who delight and disturb because they exist outside any human inventory—they're monsters of the imagination.

In his orange pants, Benya is king of a ghetto, the exact opposite of what Rosenthal claims him to be. If anything, he's an anti-Cossack. He doesn't shoot to maim or kill. Out on a raid, he orders his bandits to fire into the air. "If you don't fire in the air you may kill someone," Babel's *omniscient* narrator tells us, like a wily Talmudist commenting on his own tale.

"The King" arrived like a thunderclap in 1921. Nothing like it had ever been seen before. Babel had compressed all his childhood, all his travels, all the piebald colors of the Polish campaign, and that marvelous shorthand he'd discovered in the dreamlike sound and silence of war—"the great noiselessness of a cavalry charge"—into one story. "The King" is a war story in the slums of Odessa, a fable, a fairy tale. He would never duplicate such a melodic line again. The narrative sings to us, and we're trapped within its music as we watch tables with their velvet cloths slither across a yard, "and they sang full-throatedly, those patches of velvet, orange and red." If we talk about the wonders of the Odessa cycle, we're really talking about "The King." It's the story that introduces Benya to us . . . and Isaac Babel.

We start at a wedding in the Moldavanka. Benya is marrying off his forty-year-old sister, who suffers from a goiter, another disease of the glands, like acromegaly. He's found a "feeble youth" for her. And all the families of the Moldavanka begin with

Benya. He's the one who gives the bride away, not Papa Krik, Benya's old man. The whole of Odessa's bandit aristocracy have come to pay their respects to Benya, who's their king and their father, too.

But there's an interruption. A messenger warns the King that Odessa's new police chief intends to raid the wedding and capture all these Jewish aristocrats. It's a parody of a pogrom—a pogrom that will never happen. Benya sets the chief's own "house" and headquarters on fire, and it's like a Keystone comedy: cops with "their buttocks wiggling" rush up and down the stairs while prisoners get away. And we've entered the secret heart of the narrative, where Babel's own boyhood wish is fulfilled—that moment when he imagined himself to be a member of the Jewish Defense Corps, coalmen and horse carters like the Kriks, who fought the pogromniks but were outnumbered and couldn't win. The police had taken off their uniforms and joined the pogrom, with the tsar's consent. But it's in Odessa where the idea of a Jewish Defense Corps began. Fifty-five of these corpsmen were killed. As the American consul stationed there said after the pogrom of 1905: "Odessa presents an appearance more dead than alive."

—*more dead than alive.*

And Benya Krik (*krik* in Russian means a shout or cry), the Crier, was like the phantom voice that rose out of the carnage with its own full throat, a fairy tale king who could avenge all the killing without having to kill. We fall in love with Benya, yet we have so little of him, and like greedy children we want much more. But he escapes our grasp. And like in a dream, the narrator removes us from the wedding for a little while to tell us how Benya found his own bride—how the King fell in love with Tsilya, who appeared in her "V-necked shift" during one of his raids, when he was preparing to destroy her father, the rich man, Zender Eichbaum. Tsilya ruins his taste for plunder. He returns all the money Eichbaum has given him and asks for Tsilya's hand. "The old man had a slight stroke, but he recovered." And Benya takes his bride on a long honeymoon in Bessarabia. It's only then that he returns to marry off his sister, "a virgin of forty summers." And the story ends, as a fairy tale should, with a virgin princess entering her bridal chamber with the groom, "glaring at him carnivorously."

We meet Benya again and again in the other tales, but with each appearance he diminishes, until he's more clown than king, a comic figure in his chocolate jacket, cream pants, and raspberry boots, like some Russian candyman who drives a red car with a horn that plays *Pagliacci*. Benya is fleshed out in all his foolishness, no longer part of a fairy tale. . . .

3.

"THE POLICE END where Benya begins," sing the denizens of the Moldavanka, and that sounded fine for most of Babel's readers, seduced by that first shock of "The King." Babel was an instant hero in Odessa, where he told listeners like Paustovsky that he'd lived among the gangsters to find some coloring for his king. And Paustovsky believed how Babel had moved into a bandit's lair and had been rescued by the head of Odessa's criminal investigation division, a young man in dark-blue riding breeches who dreamt of becoming a writer, like Isaac Babel.

The mytholept was already on his way. Writing about Benya must have soothed Babel, given him a curious kind of strength. He'd created his first compelling universe, had summoned up his own magic to offer us the magic of the Moldavanka. The more famous he grew, the more the Moldavanka began to multiply with bandits until it became a Black Sea Casbah. But . . .

In 1916, before there ever was a Benya, Babel himself described the Moldavanka as "a very poor, crowded, and much suffering Jewish ghetto" without the least bit of magic ("Odessa"). And Lev Nikulin, his boyhood friend, wandered through the Moldavanka many times without meeting a king in orange pants, yet couldn't help notice the *bindyuzhniki*—those horse carters who were the only genuine counterpart to Benya. The *bindyuzhniki* were famous in Odessa, a rough lawless breed that did fight against the pogromniks and the police, but they weren't cockatoos like the Kriks. And they couldn't have organized a wedding with tablecloths that danced. Babel, Nikulin said, had created in his Odessa stories "an imaginary town, which only he could see."

And so he was lionized, first in Odessa, then in Moscow and throughout the Soviet Union. It was during NEP (1921–1928), which Lenin himself had called the "breather"—*peredyshka*—when, in spite of the battle against intellectuals, art could still flourish in a kind of boomtown atmosphere. The country had to recover from the ruins of civil war; Lenin pinched his nose like a little priest and sanctified a piecemeal return to capitalism; some farmers grew rich; black markets began to abound; gamblers, gangsters, and high-priced whores reappeared. "Moscow plunged into a life of feverish enjoyment. Foodstuffs surfaced from underground. New restaurants opened."

Babel had become the hero of this breathing period, and formalist critics like Viktor Shklovsky could talk openly in 1923 about a "geometrical style" in art and the decorative aspects of literature; and instead of brutal propaganda, a line of poetry or prose could appear in a poet's mind as an independent "patch of sound."

Shklovsky was seeking much more than the mundane, literal landscape of words. He wanted an infinity of sounds and shapes. "We live in a poor and enclosed world [. . .] We speak a pitiful language of incompletely uttered words. We look one another in the face but do not see one another."

He saw Babel as a rescuer of the Russian language. He'd known him since the days of *Letopis,* when Babel had arrived in Gorky's office like a cowboy from Odessa with a "high forehead, huge head, a face unlike a writer's," as Shklovsky wrote in *Lef* in 1924, while the *Odessa Tales* were being republished and the first stories from *Red Cavalry* began to appear.

Shklovsky reminisced about meeting him again in 1919, when Babel lived on 25th of October Street in Petersburg. "The city was beginning to be grown over, like an abandoned military camp." And Babel declared to Shklovsky "that 'nowadays' women could be had only before six since the streetcars stopped running after that."

But Babel soon disappeared, leaving behind a sweater and a

satchel for Viktor Shklovsky, who later heard that Babel had been killed while he was with the Kavalerists. The dead man resurfaced in 1924 and announced to Shklovsky with all the flavor of a mytholept that he hadn't been killed, but "[had] been beaten at great length."

No matter. Shklovsky had fallen under the sway of Benya Krik and *Red Cavalry:* "The shiniest jackboots, handsome as young girls, the whitest riding breeches, [. . .] even a fire blazing as bright as Sunday, cannot be compared to Babel's style."

Russian literature, he said, was gray as a siskin until Babel came along: Babel could speak about the stars and the clap in the same tone of voice.

But it was 1924, and the commissars had no "official" policy about literature. Even Stalin was quiet; the man with the "cockroach whiskers" was too busy consolidating his position to worry about any battle over words. But Babel had another adversary, from his days with the Cossacks. The Red Cavalry had all but disappeared, but not General Budenny, its commander-in-chief, a semiliterate anti-Semite who loved to play with language. In a letter that was published in *Oktyabr* under the title "Babizm Babelya" ["Babel's Womanly Ways"], he accused Babel of being some kind of scrub who was never even close to a battlefield, who had slandered the Cossacks, filled his writing with all sorts of erotic exercises. . . .

It was Babel's moment: he'd captivated Moscow and could do no wrong. Budenny was laughed at, but he wasn't such a bad critic. Of course, his subtext was simple: how could a *zhid* know anything about battle? Yet Budenny understood Kiril Lyutov better than a lot of Babel's more literate readers did: Babel *had* slandered the Cossacks, pieced them into his own geometric design, let Lyutov make them less than an old commander like Budenny would have liked.

But the Revolution was in dire need of a masterpiece to articulate its own music. It had one candidate: Isaac Babel. His *Red Cavalry* was as original as anything in the West, and no one in the West had been with Budenny, no one could duplicate a cavalry retreat from the point of view of a *tachanka*. No one in the West even knew what a *tachanka* was.

And so the commissars who would have loved to forget the disaster of the Polish campaign, who were deeply ambiguous about a *zhid* as their very own literary lion, were obliged to celebrate Babel. *Pravda* did chide him for writing about nurses who were whores and Cossacks who went on a rampage, but it still saluted him as Russia's rising star. . . .

Call it 1925. Babel enlists Gorky to help him get a visa for his wife. His blond beauty, Tamara Kashirina, has captured him, she a bombshell "with a pleasant husband, a small daughter, and a full social calendar." Tamara was bored, but Babel beguiled her and "her boredom vanished." He was chasing his own tail as usual, and Tamara hardly ever saw him. "In 1925 alone, Babel wrote to Tamara from seven different cities." "He would dissimulate, not only with her but with everyone, rearranging reality to fit his needs, organizing his conflicting feelings and obligations into some credible pattern," which had become his modus operandi and way of survival: Babel was everywhere and nowhere, reinventing his masks and his mindscape until his life and his fiction fed on the same reserves, and Isaac Babel was as much of a masque as Benya Krik. . . .

He publishes "The Story of My Dovecot," dedicates it to Maxim Gorky. It will begin his last major cycle of stories. He's mobbed wherever he goes.

Comes 1926. Tamara decides to have a child with Babel; their son is born in July, and Babel promptly names him Emmanuel after his own dead father. . . .

Thirty-four of his Kavalerist stories are published as a book, *Konarmia*. The West is even more unprepared for *Red Cavalry* than the Russians were—to find a voice out of the Revolution that is like a fickle whirlwind. Here was Isaac Babel offering us lyrical snapshots that were unrehearsed, as Diane Arbus would later do. It was like a revolution unto itself.

But Babel went on spinning myths. Another of Gorky's protégés, S. J. Grigorev, wrote to the grand old man in March 1926: "[Babel] has asthma. He says it's from a concussion. He plans his life on the assumption that he has five years to live." The fates would give him more than five years, and this had nothing to do with any fictional concussion. Babel's own life had already become an elaborate fiction. He'd gone back to the land of Kiril Lyutov. But he hadn't totally abandoned Benya Krik. In 1926 he would write a film script based on his *Odessa Tales*, in which he brings Benya right up to the Revolution. It was the closest thing to a novel Babel would ever write. It had, according to Cynthia Ozick, "all the surreal splendor of Babel's most plumaged prose." Eisenstein was supposed to direct *Benya Krik*. It's a pity he never did. Eisen would have given it his own kind of daring, his own kind of visual shock. In spite of all its "plumage," *Benya Krik* is a fanciful skeleton, as all good screenplays ought to be.

Written after the publication of *Red Cavalry* had made him the Revolution's most singular voice, it also reveals that he couldn't manufacture heroes who wore a Red star on their heads and danced in time to Stalin's own tune. Babel became an active screenwriter during this period. Why not? Producers ran after him, film companies courted him, directors were dying to work with him. He could secure lucrative contracts, earn money with the magic of his name—"I. Babel." His signature was like golden noise on a page. And it wasn't as if he were profligate. He had a formidable list of dependents—a mother and sister in Brussels, a wife and mother-in-law in Paris, a mistress in Moscow, assorted spongers from his Odessa days, broken-down jockeys, ex-Kavalerists. And he could wander back and forth between film studios in Moscow and the Ukraine, luxuriate in health spas for writers, occupy himself with *everything* but the swift cunning of his prose.

Benya Krik is a form of suicide, not because Benya dies, trapped within a Revolution that is worlds away from his cosmology, but because Babel ravaged his own fairy tale, sacrificed the King, surrendered him to the Revolution's song of the common man. Benya was a peacock; Benya doesn't belong in a worker's homespun paradise or in some revolutionary riddle. He's a bandit from a much more primitive period, whose only "politics" is the pogrom. The Odessa Robin Hood may extort from rich Jews, but his very presence is a warning to pogromniks—police chiefs had better stay out of the Moldavanka if they want to preserve their own buildings. All Jews, rich *and* poor, could flourish while Benya was around. . . .

But the Benya of Babel's screenplay is like Arbus' Jewish giant—a creature lost in the New World of the Russian Revolution. The Old World is Odessa itself, with its elegant cafés, like the Fankoni, one of Benya's hangouts. Benya *looks* like Benya—he plays the mandolin and wears "slick, lacquered shoes" in the screenplay—but he no longer fires in the air. The killer has learned to kill. He's not with Tsilya, the daughter of Zender Eichbaum. We never hear him speak the language of love. He's all business. And suddenly the scene shifts from 1913, when he had his own little domain, to 1919, when the Fankoni is all boarded up and a pair of bakers, Sobkov and Kochetkov, eat "ration-issue herring" and toil for the Revolution. Sobkov is a political commissar and Kochetkov is his hatchet man. Benya has also joined the Revolution. He's a chief of his own "revolutionary" regiment. But he marauds as usual, while Odessa sits in a state of paralysis, surrounded by different warring parties: the Reds, the Whites, who are still loyal to the dead tsar, the Greens (anarchists who keep switching sides), the Ukrainian Nationalists, who want a country of their own, and the foreign intervention forces, who love to meddle in Soviet affairs—the British in Archangel, the French in the Ukraine. But the French are completely baffled by all the dueling sides, and they disappear from Odessa. . . .

Meanwhile, the Ukrainians hope to bribe Benya, stuffing tsarist money inside a Torah that looks like an incredible fatted calf. And Sobkov receives a cryptic message: he's to lure the

King out of Odessa and disarm his regiment. Sobkov tricks the King, tells him that the Soviets have decided to turn his regiment into a provisions unit that can plunder for the Revolution. We catch the King riding out of Odessa on a blooded stallion, while Sobkov travels next to him on a "sleepy Siberian pony."

The bandits board a special train; some wear helmets and machine-gun belts; others march around in bare feet—Benya's ragtag army, closer to the wildness and pleasures of the imagination than to Soviet ritual and propaganda.

While Benya cavorts in a former first-class car, a gilded bathtub with the tsar's own eagles fixed to the floor, Red Army fighters climb onto the roof like angels of death.

The train arrives in a field, uncoupled from the other cars; all we have left is the locomotive and that lonesome first-class car with its gilded eagles as a reminder of the Old World. The angels of death creep down from the roof. One of Benya's bandits tries to escape. Kochetkov shoots him in the head. Then he choreographs the King's own execution. He takes Benya's hand, and like a partner in some slow dance he spins Benya around, so that the King faces him. And someone shoots, either a soldier or Kochetkov himself. A spot appears on the back of Benya's shaved neck, "a gaping wound with blood spurting in all directions."

But the story doesn't end there; we learn that the orders to isolate Benya and execute him came from the chairman of the Odessa Executive Committee, just as a similar chairman from the same committee had "lent" Isaac Babel to the Red Cavalry as Kiril Lyutov; Babel himself is embedded in the screenplay like some unfortunate ghost *and* pilgrim.

4.

BENYA KRIK WAS released in 1927 and the Party apparatus soon plucked it out of circulation. An old-world gangster wasn't a suitable subject in a Soviet Union that believed in garage mechanics and baker-commissars like Kochetkov. . . .

Babel continues to wander. He talks of a novel he's writing about the Cheka—he goes deeper and deeper into the Devil's mouth. There are tales and rumors of Babel sitting down with the secret police, prying, pressing, as inquisitive as ever. He will brag to Osip and Nadezhda Mandelstam how he "spent all his time meeting militiamen"—Chekists—and drinking with them. Osip asks him why he's so drawn to these *militiamen.* "[W]as it a desire to see what it was like in the exclusive store where the merchandise is death? Did he just want to touch it with his fingers? 'No,' Babel replied, 'I don't want to touch it with my fingers—I just want to have a sniff and see what it smells like.' "

He visits France in '27, boasts about his former service with the Cheka and about the novel he is writing, but Zhenya will later tell Nathalie that there was no such novel—or, at least, he hadn't confided in her. And even if he had envisioned such a novel, would it have concerned the adventures of Kiril Lyutov inside the Lubyanka? Babel himself had become the Jewish giant in the photograph, powerless and puffed up.

He grows listless in Paris, as if he were living in some strange swamp. In March 1928 he writes to I. Livshits, a boyhood friend: "What I am going through must be called by its proper name—it's an illness, neurasthenia, like the one in the days of my youth."

But he didn't have a dovecote to comfort him, or that mysterious rot of the Moldavanka, a Moldavanka where his grandmother lived and where he could watch those magnificent draymen, who must have been as exotic as Jewish acrobats for a sickly boy. . . .

He lingers in France, visits Marseilles, which reminds him of the Moldavanka, and the longer he's away, the more other Soviet writers begin to carp—*Babel has abandoned the Soviets; Babel is a slave of the West.* He returns in October 1928, with little to show for his fifteen months abroad. But he's come back to a much different Soviet Union. That Russian Wild West is gone. Stalin has strangled Lenin's "breather," and will introduce the "great breaking point," where all Soviet citizens have to become *udarniki*—shock troops—on that sacrificial highway called socialism.

A born battler, Budenny senses that it's the opportune moment to revive his attack on Babel. And Gorky has given him the occasion. In an article about the craft of writing, Gorky declares: "Comrade Budenny has pounced upon Babel's *Red Cavalry* and I don't believe he should have, because Budenny himself likes to embellish the outside not only of his men, but of his horses too." Budenny counterattacks; in an open letter to the grand old man of Soviet literature, he starts to complain: Babel was never an active soldier, Babel "hung around with some unit deep in the rear."

Babel is "an erotomanic author" who observed the Cossacks through his own morbid prism, concentrating on bare breasts in field kitchens and in the forest. His book should be called *In the Backwaters of the Red Cavalry.*

But Gorky is as much a battler as Budenny and even more beloved. He publishes an open letter in *Pravda. Red Cavalry,* he says, "has no parallel in Russian literature." He appeals to Stalin, asks the Boss to end the quarrel, and the Boss obliges. "*Red Cavalry* is not so bad as all that. It is a very good book."

And the carping stops. Russia's chief literary critic has spoken. The case against *Red Cavalry* is closed, as long as Stalin needs Gorky, and Gorky can stay alive. . . .

5.

CALL IT 1930. There's more and more pressure on Babel to find a Soviet subject that will recapture the romance of Benya Krik. A writer who can't produce is nothing but a parasite. Babel plans to resurrect Benya as Kolya Topuz, another bandit, but one who is much more pliable, like a tamed bear with a ring in its nose. He starts a novella about a reformed Odessa gangster, calls it *Kolya Topuz* in honor of his new hero. "I want to show how this sort of man adapts to Soviet reality." Kolya works on a collective farm, but "since he has the mentality of a gangster, he's constantly breaking out of the limits of ordinary life, which leads to numerous funny situations."

But not into myth. We don't have a line of Babel's novella. He may have been working on *Kolya* at the time of his arrest. *Kolya* could be one of his lost manuscripts. But somehow I don't believe it. Babel would visit collective farm after collective farm, would even write about kolkhozniks, but the only kolkhozniks who really interest him are hunchbacks and whores, and whores had no place on a collective farm. . . .

In "Gapa Guzhva," an acrobatic widow who drinks vodka on a roof and has tumbled into bed with every single male in her village is the scourge of all the village wives. A judge in a shabby coat has come to Velikaya Krinitsa to examine its little crimes and misdemeanors—"all the wounds, visible and invisible," including Gapa Guzhva. The village elders won't let her join the collective farm. "Judge," she asks, "what's going to happen to the whores?"

"They will no longer exist."

That judge in his shabby little coat could have been sentencing Babel himself. There was no room for gargoyles in Stalin's big collective farm, only for shock troops with a bullet-headed devotion to the State.

—*They will no longer exist.*

The Russian Association of Proletarian Writers (RAPP), ruled by Leopold Leopoldovich Averbakh, was sick of "fellow travelers" like Isaac Babel who could not commit to the Party and the virtues of "proletarian" literature. Averbakh was a madman, a militant, and a conniving hack, but he'd become a dictator, right under Stalin himself. It was Averbakh's brainstorm to send writers into factories and collective farms to uncover and unleash the talent buried within the proletariat. Babel had to acquiesce, fulfill his duties as a "soldier" from RAPP; not a single proletarian writer was ever discovered by Averbakh and his mission of madmen. . . .

Meanwhile, Babel shuffled along, making friends with "engineers, jockeys, cavalrymen, architects, bee-keepers, cymbalists." He grew more secretive—"his days were like the tunnelings of a mole"—and silent. And, for the first time since his apprentice year in Petersburg, he wrote stories that were being refused by Soviet editors.

But at least he was able to articulate his own dilemma. "As long as I don't publish I am merely accused of laziness. If, on the other hand, I publish, then a veritable avalanche of weighty and dangerous accusations will descend upon my head. I feel like a beautiful girl at a ball, with whom everyone wishes to dance. If I were to let myself be persuaded, however, the entire gathering, like a single person, would instantly turn against me. . . . To dance at this ball as I do—this is surely a provocative impropriety, a wild and dangerous example."

And Babel was slowly silenced, like that beauty at the ball. He'd danced like an amazing dervish for a little while, obliging us to follow him with our own blind faith. And then he stopped in front of Stalin's wall. The little commissars of the Revolution had plucked off all his plumage, until he was one more Jewish giant, lantern-jawed and weak within a terrifying enfeeblement of language that strangled an entire country and left Babel a "dead soul" long before the Cheka came to collect him.

ZHENYA AT A SUMMER RESORT IN BELGIUM, CIRCA 1928

Chapter Six

MAKHNO AND MAUPASSANT

1.

N JULY 2003 I went on a pilgrimage to Washington, D.C., to interview Nathalie Babel. I didn't know what to expect when I knocked on Nathalie's door. Should I call her "Natasha," the name under which Babel had known his little Russian daughter who happened to have been born in France? I admired her fierce devotion. She'd become Babel's "editor" in the United States, had gathered his stories and letters . . . like a cunning cadet.

"Being Russian, French, American, and Jewish has meant that wherever I am, part of me could be somewhere else." She could also have been writing about her father, who was always "somewhere else," whether in his own mind or on some crazy gallop from place to place, or about wanderers like myself who'd traveled from their own "Odessa" on some rocking horse of words.

I felt close to Nathalie. Was she really the child of that Headless Man? When she opened the door I didn't have any doubt. She looked like Babel, had the wondrous truculence of her father's face, like a little commissar of mind and imagination. I'd been told she was a tough customer. Nathalie herself had said on the phone that she'd scared off another interviewer. He'd come all the way from Montreal and wanted to camp outside her apartment, question her for ten hours at a clip. But his first question was fatal. "Who are the Shapochnikoffs?" he asked. (Shapochnikoff was Maria Babel's married name.) But I had studied the whole Babel tree, including the Shvevels (his mother's family), the Gronfeins (his first wife's family), and the Shapochnikoffs.

I asked Nathalie about her mother, Zhenya Gronfein.

"She's the one who intrigues me," I said, the dark lady from Kiev (with reddish brown hair), who'd been dismissed by Ilya Ehrenburg and others as a bourgeois beauty. The entire Soviet Union, it seems, had condemned her because her father happened to be rich before the Revolution. She'd been written out of Babel's life, expunged. We have Antonina Pirozhkova's testimony, her years with Babel—the pieces of string, Babel's fear of forests (was he still haunted by the Red Cavalry campaigns near the end of his life?)—but we have nothing from the first Mrs. Babel, who was so unlike the second. . . .

Nathalie would grow up without the usual children's stories. She had Isaac Babel. "Mother read the stories to me as a child. She admired them very much." It wasn't only Antonina who recalled Babel's piece of string. Zhenya had told Nathalie about that habit of his. "They were in the Caucasus [it was 1922]. He would work at night, with a piece of string, and every day he would read to her what he was working on."

Zhenya had fond memories of Batum, where she lived with Babel on the side of a mountain and had to hike for miles on unsafe roads in order to reach the nearest market. There were "hard times" on Babel's mountain, yet "they were happy together." An "heiress" from Kiev, "she didn't have the slightest idea of how to cook. But she decided she had to cook." And when she made Babel soup for the first time, "he put his knife into it. The knife stood up in the soup."

Babel worked like a madman on his mountain. And then there was the move to Moscow when his writing began to unravel. Enter Tamara Kashirina, the Russian Delilah who entangled herself with the weak-eyed Samson of Soviet literature. And Babel scrawled his *Avtobiographiya* that same year: 1924. It begins to make sense why he didn't include his marriage to Zhenya, a daughter of the Jewish bourgeoisie. He'd had his second birth, as a Soviet writer like Kiril Lyutov, who'd also "lost" a wife. The nom de guerre he used was hardly an accident—*lyuty* in Russian means "wild, ferocious," as if Babel were pretending to be "ferocious" as a Cossack, or as "wild" as language itself, or could borrow his persona from the Revolution, cut off the past with some of the same violence. But the man who rode with the Cossacks wore an invisible skullcap. He had a tribe as compelling as the Cossacks themselves. . . .

Zhenya couldn't forget the string of pearls her father hid from the Bolsheviks. Gronfein "twisted that string of pearls into the electric cord hanging from the ceiling. [And he did it just before the era] of Bolsheviks entering your house and grabbing everything—muzhiks coming in and threatening everybody," after 1917. Her father "died first and quickly." Zhenya had already gone to France, where she had neither friends nor family, and she asked Babel to bring her "certain mementos" of her dead father; Babel found "two small ivory cigarette holders—that's all."

2.

I HAD TO trace the path of the two ivory pieces. So I'm on a second pilgrimage—to the land of Maupassant, looking for Babel's first address in Paris: Villa Chauvelot. But Villa Chauvelot has disappeared from the map. And so I wander into some labyrinth at the edge of Paris, in the Fifteenth Arrondissement, right near the *périphérique,* a sinister road that circles Paris like a hangman's knot. Babel's old neighborhood is in a *bidonville* where boulevards float into nothingness. I find the rue Chauvelot, which must have contained its own cul-de-sac, a blind alley with little houses where Babel had lived at number 15, but the whole "Villa" has been swallowed up by a modern housing development with broken balconies at the corner of the street. I reconnoiter on the rue Chauvelot like a Cossack commander, circle around the street to the impasse du Labrador, another cul-de-sac, which butts into the side wall of the housing project. I want to explore a bit, to uncover traces of Babel's blind alley, but a wolfhound sits deep within the impasse and stares at me with his Siberian eyes, and I'm obliged to retreat. . . .

Babel left for Paris in July 1927 and didn't return until October of the following year. Was he seeking some sort of reconciliation with Zhenya? A Headless Man capable of multiple lives (with multiple women), he arrived with his mother-in-law, Berta Davidovna, like a Russian Yankee Doodle prepared to conquer Paris. He lived among the "deaf-mutes," as the Soviets called capitalists in the West, for fifteen months, a dangerously long time, even for a writer of Babel's repute, a writer with a wife already in France (since December 1925), and a mother and sister in Belgium. It looked like the intrigue of an exile, someone who was planning to stay among the "deaf-mutes." And indeed, exile must have been on Babel's mind. French was his own first love. Hadn't he announced himself as the new Maupassant? Hadn't he visited Paris in his psyche long before he arrived, crowing to his writer friends about the frilly pink lampshades of Maupassant's last flat? He was fluent in French since his days at Nicholas I, when Monsieur Vadon must have made him feel like a little Monte Cristo who had to return to his "homeland." And he was lonely, often desperate, without his mother and sister near him. He would become crazed whenever letters didn't arrive. "Write, write, write" is the chronic complaint in his own letters. "You're knifing me."

What kind of welcome could he have hoped for in France? He'd been living on and off with Tamara, had a "love child" to legitimize their liaison. Yet Zhenya, the little bourgeoise, as Ilya Ehrenburg called her, did welcome him back. She would tremble before he arrived, with anticipation *and* anger probably, over his love affairs (there was more than one Tamara) and the birth of the little boy. Zhenya would have known about the child, no matter how evasive Babel was: Moscow was a land of blabbermouths. And Zhenya kept that secret from Nathalie herself. It was only in 1957, when she was dying in a public ward in Paris, that she opened up to Nathalie.

"I left Russia mostly because of an affair your father was having with an actress, a very beautiful woman. She pursued him relentlessly, and didn't care that he was married. She wanted him and his fame, and had a son by him. Perhaps one day you might meet this man, and you should know he is your half-brother and not someone you could fall in love with."

Why did she play Cassandra on her deathbed? Zhenya must have been carrying that same wound for thirty years; the reality of little Mischa (or Emmanuel) disturbed her much more than any mistress. And so she obsessed that Nathalie might fall in love with her half brother, as if she imagined parts for Nathalie and Mischa in some Sophoclean drama. But Nathalie wasn't living in Moscow; there was little chance she would ever meet that anonymous boy. And yet the possibility plagued Zhenya like a little tale of incest. How many times must she have imagined that boy, wished to annihilate him, or steal him from Tamara? And it was into this imbroglio that Babel crept, the infected husband who was already notorious among Russian émigrés as the man who swore he'd served in the Cheka.

We have no diaries or agendas of Babel's day-to-day existence in Paris. We know that he met Feodor Chaliapin in 1927, and that Chaliapin, the most adored actor-singer of his era, complained to Babel of his own unhappiness and neglect. And Babel

felt the same neglect as Chaliapin. He was only a "skeleton" in
Paris, one more Soviet writer in a land where writers weren't
treated like national treasures or holy men. No one stopped him
in the cafés, demanded his autograph. No one talked like Benya
Krik. He would hike to Montparnasse from the Villa Chauvelot,
sit in the Dôme or the Coupole with his émigré friends, such as
Boris Souvarine, a charter member of the French Communist
Party until he was kicked out in 1924, and Yuri Annenkov, a celebrated painter and portraitist, and he would grumble to them
about his disenchantment with the Revolution, but everybody
grumbled. The Cheka could have been sitting with him at the
Coupole. Tsarist generals were kidnapped right off the streets of
Paris. . . .

Did Babel's jeremiads mean that he intended to elope *permanently* to Paris? In letters to his mother and Maria he harps
about Zhenya's playboy brother, Lyova, who was on the verge of
becoming an American millionaire. And Babel had to wait until
Lyova's situation became solid. "This is a very important point
in planning our future existence." But Lyova's situation would
never become solid. He was always about to sign some contract
with an American mogul. And Babel waits and waits. "No news
from Lyova at all." It seems odd that Babel counted on this phantom brother to deliver him from the bondage of being poor in
Paris, like some totem or symbolic wish that would have allowed
him to break with the Soviets, be near Maria and his mother,
mend his marriage . . .

Zhenya didn't leave any portraits of Babel in Paris, but his
old school chum Lev Nikulin did. Nikulin happened to be in

Paris at the same time as Isaac Babel. "On his first visit to Paris, Babel seemed to melt into the background of the city. He soon lost interest in Montparnasse, the Coupole, and the Dôme [Hemingway's hangout], and would often come to see us on the Avenue de Wagram, or rather on the rue Bréa [Nikulin means the rue Brey], where, in the cheap Hôtel Tilsit[t], all kinds of people lived—Russians and various foreigners of no fixed occupation."

Babel kept to his mysterious, mandarin ways. He wouldn't phone in advance. He'd appear at the hotel without warning, capture Nikulin, oblige him to trek across Paris. They stopped in front of a bordello one morning in Montmartre, looked through the windows at the debris inside. Babel wanted to know if the bordello kept its own books. "It would be fascinating to study the entries in the books. They would make a chapter in a good novel," one that Babel himself might have written, with its own stark geometry—mirrors, money, and lace pants. . . .

And then there was Volodya—a Russian taxi driver who also lived at the Tilsitt. "In autumn, in bad weather, he didn't have much business and he'd drive us round the city at half price. We would go along slowly, stopping by the Seine, or in the Latin Quarter, or the ancient little square at the back of the Panthéon." They would observe Paris in the "eerie, phosphorescent glow" of the gaslights. And years later, Babel would recall these "nocturnal trips" and say to Nikulin: "How nice it would be to go for a ride with Volodya again."

His friends in Moscow mistook the Villa Chauvelot for some luxurious mansion in the middle of Paris, but Babel had to shrink within the walls of his cul-de-sac. "I lead a most simple life," he explained to one of these friends. "I write. I can't sit for more than three francs' worth of coffee. I don't have much money. There's nothing to have a good time on. I walk around the streets of Paris and look closely at everything. I avoid old acquaintances and don't look for new ones. I go to bed at eleven and that turns out to be late."

"[I]t is clear that settling down in the West would not have suited Babel," says Lev Nikulin. Babel "could not do without the hectic, helter-skelter life of the country that was dearest to him." But Nikulin himself had returned to Moscow. Souvarine and Annenkov did not, and they could feel the frustration in Babel. "Here [in Paris] a taxi driver has more freedom than the rector of a Soviet university," he said to Annenkov.

Babel was waiting for some deliverer. "I can't sleep nights. I have a terrible cold, my eye is all puffed up and full of matter. All in all, I am decomposing even less aesthetically than the Paris bourgeoisie."

He loved to send notes to Nikulin via the *pneu* (or *pneumatique*), that French postal service whereby letters whisked across Paris by an underground system of compressed-air tubes, a system that must have seemed perfect for such a subterranean man. He was suffocating within the mask of Kiril Lyutov again. He couldn't seem to put on the right pose in Paris. Odessan gangster, cavalry officer, Chekist, expatriate, or proud Soviet writer? Kiril was homesick. "Spiritual life is nobler in Russia," he wrote to his friend Livshits in October 1927. "I am poisoned by Russia, I long for it, I think only of Russia." Or, as the critic Milton

Ehre tells us, trying to make up Babel's mind for him: "Russia was tiresome and frightening, but it was also the battleground of history. Paris was a holiday."

And I suppose it was, but I suspect that Babel was already sick of battlefields. He had to go home. He couldn't support himself or his family in France. It was on his return to Moscow that he started *Kolya Topuz*, his novel about an Odessa bandit who was as problematic as Babel himself. . . .

3.

BUT SOMETHING HAPPENED during his last weeks in Paris. Zhenya became pregnant, Zhenya would bear him a child. His daughter, Nathalie or Natasha, was born on July 17, 1929. "She [Zhenya] carried the child for eleven months, unless it is the pregnancy of a railroad conductor," Babel wrote to Maria. He would talk about Natasha as "the foundling girl," but he was obsessed with her from the moment of her birth. "I have become steadier, calmer, harder, and I am ripe for family life." He longed to bring his "little (but enlarged) family" back to Russia. Zhenya didn't share his longing. She was much more prescient about the Soviet Union than her husband, who was too caught up in being Isaac Babel, the ex-cavalier. . . .

The bureaucrats told him he couldn't travel abroad until his productivity increased like some magnificent diesel, but the productivity they wanted was a full-throated hymn to the Revolution, with an endless ride on Stalin's propaganda train, and all Babel could produce were oblique songs about his childhood, or about some whore who was as much of an outlaw as Benya Krik. And so he retreated to a horse farm, met Antonina Pirozhkova in Moscow (it was 1932), and told her "how difficult it had been for him to get permission to go abroad and how long the process had dragged on." But he continued to live in his own little dream of a Soviet hearth. "I'm going there to meet a little three-year-old French miss [Nathalie]. I'd like to bring her back to Russia, as I fear they might turn her into a monkey there."

And finally, in September 1932, the Soviet "castle" granted Petitioner Babel the privilege of seeing his little daughter in France. It would remain the single most significant event in his life, a kind of mutual seduction that was beyond any of his masks . . . or powers as a mytholept. All his poses were idle with Nathalie. She devoured whatever space he had. "I still haven't recovered from the shock I received at the sight of my daughter—I never suspected anything of this sort," he writes to Maria on September 19, a little after his arrival. "It is really quite beyond me where she could have got so much cunning, liveliness and cupidity [from her father, of course]. And it is all full of style and charm. . . . I haven't been able to find one ounce of meekness or shyness in this tiny tiger cub."

"I have sired a tiger," he continues on September 25. But he couldn't utterly cure his mythomania. A kind of nagging yet playful insecurity would begin over Zhenya's prolonged pregnancy. "Now, inasmuch as she [Nathalie] was born ten days after the time limit and inasmuch as Makhno resides in Paris, I no longer have any doubt left that it is he who is her father."

Makhno had a special meaning for Babel. It was Makhno

who had destroyed the advantage of an army on horseback, Makhno who was the first real genius of the *tachanka*. He hid his firepower in little haycarts, and no infantry or cavalry in the world could defeat his mounted machine guns. "Makhno, as Protean as Nature itself" ("Discourse on the *Tachanka*"). He was a Ukrainian guerrilla who fought against the Reds with his own anarchist band. Babel admired his boldness and his bravery. Makhno was also very cruel—it's men from his band who rape the Jewish maid in "Makhno's Boys." He fled to Paris after the Civil War. And he would occupy Babel's mind as an unstoppable force, cruel as creativity.

Babel's daughter was another unstoppable force, and he dubbed her Makhno—"In the last few days, Makhno has quieted down and sometimes displays such meekness and reasonableness that my heart melts."

He went everywhere with Makhno, was her constant squire. "I have no time to myself because I must escort my daughter: tomorrow she goes to some birthday party; on Saturday, she has a Christmas party in her kindergarten."

But pretty soon Babel began to chase his own tail. He was still depending on Lyova for some magical bailout. Meanwhile, he had trouble writing. "It seems quite impossible for me to get down to work here and that depresses me very much." He became friendly with Ilya Ehrenburg, whom he'd first met in Moscow after *Red Cavalry* had created such a storm. "Man lives for the pleasure of sleeping with a woman, of eating ices on a hot day," Babel had told him then. Now he talked of his tiger cub—little Makhno. But it was Ehrenburg who had penetrated Babel's masks, who saw beneath the swagger: Babel, he said, "was a sad person who was able to laugh."

He couldn't be without his daughter, yet he couldn't keep her with him. He'd received "a strange summons from Moscow." And his fellow writers had been circulating "[a]ll sorts of absurd but sinister rumors" about him. They were jealous of Babel, *meanly* jealous, and began telling tales about him to the Cheka, that he intended to "vanish," live permanently in the West. "I'm glad I'm going to Moscow. All the rest is bitter and uncertain," Babel wrote to Annenkov.

But how glad could he have been? "My native land greeted me with autumn, poverty and what she alone has for me—poetry." But he would have to live without the poetry of Makhno. Nothing could hold him for very long, not even his little retreat at Molodenovo, where he could "handle" as many horses as he liked. He moved into a Cossack settlement, going from one isolated place to the next. "I am living in peace and warmth. . . . The only thing is that I can't get my daughter out of my heart." Back in Moscow in February 1934, he writes to Maria: "I think of Natasha a thousand times a day and my heart contracts."

That April he writes to his mother about the "paradoxical thing" of his existence as a Soviet writer—"in our country, which is still so poor, I live in greater comfort and *freedom* than you and Zhenya. When it comes to apartments, food, services, warmth and peace—I can have it all." He's blinded himself enough to believe that his wife, daughter, mother, sister, and her doctor husband, Grisha, would all be better off with him in some stupendous household near his horse farm, and if not, what can he do? The bureaucrats won't let him out of their little paradise to visit Zhenya and Natasha in Paris. And then fate intervenes in the figure of André Malraux, who has organized his own "International Congress [of anti-Fascist Writers] for the Defense of Culture and Peace," in 1935. But when Malraux realizes that the two Russian writers he admired most—Babel and Boris Pasternak—are not among the Soviet delegates, he screams to Stalin himself (via the Soviet embassy in Paris). A Soviet air force plane is immediately commandeered, but Pasternak is too sick to fly. He's hiding at a clinic, in the midst of a physical and mental collapse. And Babel decides to accompany him to the Congress by train.

Pasternak and Babel arrive on the third day. It's June. Paris is caught in a heat wave. Pasternak sits like a ghost, but Babel is the star of a congress that includes E. M. Forster, Bertolt Brecht, Robert Musil, André Gide, Bertrand Russell, and Virginia Woolf. *Red Cavalry* has appeared in translation, and the other delegates can appreciate his "plumage"; they greet him with great warmth. He charms them in "masterly French," speaks for fifteen minutes without a prepared speech, but doesn't for a moment forget the tightrope he is on. He's giving a performance, and he has to make the delegates laugh. He talks of the collective farmer who has bread, a house, even a decoration. "But it's not enough for him. Now he wants poetry to be written about him."

Can Malraux and the other delegates catch the bitterness underlying Babel's little joke? They envision Stalin as the wise monk who never travels, who leads the fight against fascism from within the Kremlin's walls. "For us now the USSR presents a spectacle of incomparable importance and great hope," says Gide. Only in Russia "are there real readers"—Stalin's readers. Stalin, Babel understands, was the collective farmer and *mad monk* who hurled language and laws "like horseshoes at the head." Stalin was the ultimate poet, who used language to reward and to kill on a "collective farm" that covered two continents. . . .

Babel meets with the delegates. He performs, he dances, he runs home to Zhenya and Makhno, who's almost six. "I feel great. I find I am the father of an infant who is notorious for her criminal activities within a range of ten kilometers."

He's also planning to write. "I'll spend the short time assigned to me in Paris in roaming around the place in search of material like a hungry wolf."

But he couldn't understand that the hungry wolf was feeding on its own flesh, and there was even too little of that. He'd begun to dismiss *Red Cavalry* as a tale about horses. Like Mark Twain, who would dismiss *Huckleberry Finn* as a humdrum book for boys, Babel was unconscious of his strengths and sources, had no idea what could ignite him and what could not. The explosion of form would only come when an inner search clung to an outer one, when Mark Twain captured his boyhood on the Mississippi through Huck Finn, and Babel created his own world through the "flesh" of the Moldavanka. He could find no internal music for all his subsequent wanderings in the Ukraine, all his stopovers at a Cossack settlement. Babel's fire came from certain erotic moments he'd suffered through as a boy (hinted at in "First Love"), suffered like slaps on the face, and *Red Cavalry* was a wondrous, deepening spiral because Kiril Lyutov wore the mask that a boy might wear—he was a boy's hollowed-out impression of a man. . . .

Babel continues to scheme. He begins assembling exit visas for his tribe. "The prospects of my family's settling in the USSR are very bright now and I enriched the Soviet Union with a new citizen when Natasha was entered on Zhenya's new passport." But by August he was gone, without his family. And now his whole life would become more and more of a mask. He will travel with Antonina, begin living with her, but can never mention her in his letters, so that what he writes to Maria and his mother becomes a piece of fiction. He visits Odessa with Antonina, gets Maria's favorite poppy-seed bagels from a shop near Gorky Street, but he can't declare whom he had the bagels with; Antonina herself is a strange "cutout" in his correspondence, an absent detail that destroys the very message.

He's mobbed wherever he goes in Odessa. "Completely unknown street cleaners, news vendors and what not, come up to me in the street, say hello and engage me in the most incredible conversations." And when he comes out of a theater, hordes of young people block the way to his automobile. . . .

Even with all the adulation, he can't really return to Odessa. The Moldavanka was the land of memory, where his imagination could dwell. But it wasn't a home. *There is no there there,* Gertrude Stein once said, and Gertrude wasn't wrong. When Alexander Blok, Russia's great symbolist poet, was arrested by the Cheka in 1919, he sat in the same cell with a bunch of monarchists and Mensheviks who argued relentlessly about Russia's future. And Blok had only this to say: "But where will the artist, with his homeless craft, go to in your future?"

4.

BABEL MAY HAVE walked Paris, but he was no *flâneur,* like Walter Benjamin or Baudelaire. Benjamin was a pathfinder who could feel the lyrical pull between epochs, fall upon arcades or wounded stones in Paris or Marseilles, discover the design of the nineteenth century embedded in the twentieth. His home was the library he carried from place to place, with the quotations he would cram into every text like some moveable mosaic. Babel wasn't of the same priesthood.

The two stories he wrote about Paris, "Dante Street" (1934) and "The Trial" (1938), read like bits of a travelogue, or the journal of someone stuck in a place he doesn't want to be. "There is no solitude more deadly than solitude in Paris," says the nameless narrator of "Dante Street," who wears the trappings of Isaac Babel. "For all those who come from afar this town is a form of exile." In "The Trial," Ivan Nedachin, a former lieutenant colonel with the Whites, who has wandered from Zagreb to Paris, where he couldn't pass the taxi driver test, becomes a gigolo and a jewel thief. The daughter-in-law of his last victim goes to the police. Nedachin is arrested in a Montparnasse wine cellar "where Moscow gypsies sang." At criminal court a gendarme pushes him "out into the light, as a bear is pushed into a circus arena." He is a bear, but from some unknown circus. "He towered over the crowd—helpless, large, with dangling arms—like an animal from another world."

Babel was this same animal, and not because of Paris. Paris becomes a macabre stand-in for the feeling of *foreignness* in his own psyche. . . .

Babel's best story about Paris takes place in Petersburg. Published in 1932 (like "Argamak"), it has ambiguous antecedents. Babel would have us believe that he composed "Guy de Maupassant" between 1920 and 1922. But I'd swear it couldn't have been written, or greatly revised, until after his first trip to France. Cynthia Ozick calls the story "a cunning seriocomic sexual fable fixed on the weight and trajectory of language itself." It's also Babel's most disturbing autobiography.

The narrator, whose fortunes are closely linked to Babel's, finds himself in Petersburg in 1916 with a forged passport and without a penny. He's twenty years old and he's taken in by Alexey Kazantsev, a teacher of Russian literature whose real passion is Spain. "Kazantsev had never so much as passed through Spain, but his love for that country filled his whole being."

Babel has visited upon Kazantsev his own puppy love for France. He appears like a ghostly fragment inside all the main characters—as if they (and we ourselves) were swimming with Isaac Babel in the underbelly of a dream. . . .

The narrator refuses to become a clerk: "[B]etter starve, go to jail, or become a bum than spend ten hours a day behind a desk in an office." And this credo feeds Babel's own mythology, testifies to his acumen as the barefoot boy who rushes from one

adventure to the next. "This wisdom of my ancestors was firmly
lodged in my head: we are born to enjoy our work, our fights,
and our love: we are born for that and for nothing else."

But his ancestors were locked within the ghetto wall, a pale
that would have broken his ancestors' back, and that delivered
little love or joy. Yet our picaro rushes out to collect whatever he
can. Bendersky, the Jewish banker-lawyer who owns a publishing house, has decided to republish all of Maupassant, with his
wife, Raïsa, as translator. Raïsa can't make her translations work,
and Kasantsev recommends the narrator.

He arrives at the Benderskys' in a borrowed coat. They live
in a mansion near the Moyka River. A high-breasted maid greets
him at the door. "In her open gray eyes one saw a petrified lewd-
ness. She moved slowly. I thought: when she makes love she
must move with unheard-of agility."

The maid's imagined acrobatics are like the flights of power
in Babel's art—that movement from inertia into an acrobat of
image and sound. . . .

But it's Raïsa who occupies our mind, and not the maid.
"Maupassant," she tells the boy, "is the only passion of my life,"
and Babel might well have been looking at his own face in the
mirror—she's the erotic monstrosity of *his* lifelong passion for
Maupassant.

But there's little of Maupassant in Raïsa's translations—all
she has is "something loose and lifeless, the way Jews wrote
Russian in the old days," *before* Isaac Babel.

The boy brings Raïsa's translations home to Kasantsev's
attic and cuts his way through "the tangled undergrowth of her

prose." And it's Babel who's speaking here, not the picaro. "A phrase is born into the world both good and bad at the same time. The secret lies in a slight, an almost invisible twist. The lever should rest in your hand, getting warm, and you can only turn it once, not twice."

All his life, Babel worked at that "almost invisible twist." Raïsa and the boy are the twin demons that haunted Babel, one pulling toward access and jungle growth, and the other toward a surgical *pinch* of every line.

The boy returns to Raïsa with the corrected manuscript. Raïsa is overwhelmed: "the lace between her constricted breasts danced and heaved," like language itself. One evening he finds the Benderskys at dinner. He listens to their "neighing laughter," which serves as a marvelous counter to the dignified Russian he studied at school. What he hears is "a Jewish noise, rolling and tripping and ending up on a melodious, singsong note," like the noise of the Moldavanka. . . .

Raïsa comes to him drunk. "I want to work," she says, while "the nipples rose beneath the clinging silk" of her sacklike gown. They drink her husband's most expensive wine. And they start on Raïsa's translation of "L'Aveu" ("The Confession"), about a coachman, Hippolyte, and a farmer girl with "mighty calves"— always an aphrodisiac for Babel—and all the cat-and-mouse of seduction. After two years the girl gives in; the coachman sleeps with her right inside his carriage, under "the gay sun of France," with a sick old nag leading them along. . . .

The boy takes his courage from the story. He kisses Raïsa on the lips. She presses herself against the wall. "Of all the gods ever put on the crucifix, this was the most ravishing."

Does the narrator make love to her or not? He leaves that mansion on the Moyka before Raïsa's husband returns from the theater. But the language of his little walk seems to support the notion that he hasn't been quite as lucky as Hippolyte. "Monsters roamed behind the boiling walls. The roads amputated the legs of those walking on them," as all godlike, gorgeous women with a pink layer of fat on their bellies amputate husbands and suitors who are frightened of their sex.

Frustrated, the narrator returns to the attic and starts to read a book on Maupassant's life and work. Attacked by congenital syphilis at twenty-five. Incredible creativity and joie de vivre. His sight weakens. He suffers from headaches and fits of hypochondria. Suspicious of everyone, he dashes about the Mediterranean in a yacht, runs to Morocco. Famous at an early age, he cuts his throat at forty, survives, is locked in a madhouse. He crawls about on his hands and knees, "devouring his own excrement." Monsieur de Maupassant is turning into an animal, reads his hospital report. He dies at forty-two, his mother surviving him. And once again Babel goes into his little act of trying to grasp something prescient in the last line of a story: "My heart contracted as the foreboding of some essential truth touched me with light fingers."

The fingers weren't light at all. The narrator *and* the author are terrified. The arc of Maupassant's life may *seem* to duplicate Babel's: early fame and quick decline. But there's a much stronger parallel than Babel might have been conscious of. Maupassant hadn't been the only one to devour excrement. Perhaps he had to devour before he could create. Images of excrement overwhelm *Red Cavalry:* fields are strewn with excrement, and the old man who has his throat cut in "Crossing into Poland" lies in his own filth. Excrement is a strange, vital force of the ghetto itself—part of its magic decay. And rather than the chronicle of a death foretold (Babel's own), "Guy de Maupassant" is about an author-magician who *lent* Babel a language and a country and a totemic town—Paris—that would inspire Babel, free him to build his own myths as a writer, even if he couldn't really live there. Perhaps no town could ever match the dream he had of Maupassant.

Chapter Seven

FINAL FICTION

1.

T HE LAST YEARS, the lonely years, as Stalin tightened his noose—what could it have been like for Babel after he came home from France? It was August 1935. He'd lingered for two months with Zhenya and Makhno, while the other Soviet delegates at Malraux's little congress, who didn't have a wife and daughter in Paris and were scared to death of Stalin and his phobia of *anything* foreign, returned as fast as they could. I suspect Babel was a sleepwalker for the remainder of his life, but he was still a minor deity in the Writers Union, part of a privileged caste in a "new Moscow," where "people were opening up their first bank accounts, buying furniture and writing novels." Babel had a big Ford, a chauffeur, servants; he could eat at "closed" restaurants and travel wherever he wanted within the Soviet Union; and he would soon have a dacha built for him at Peredelkino—

but he was like a great musician being forced to fiddle, and he couldn't fiddle hard enough or long enough to satisfy his Soviet keepers.

Pirozhkova would have us remember a serene and saintly Babel, "born for merriment." But there were no more meadows in May, bisected by an angelic band of women and horses. I'm not convinced there ever were, except in Babel's mind. Georgy Munblit, the editor of a Soviet literary magazine, recalls a writer "about whose protracted silence in the thirties there were newspaper articles and feuilletons, speeches and writers' conferences, and even, apparently, satirical songs," but behind the mask of silence "was a man with an almost morbid sense of responsibility"—responsibility toward everyone but himself. As writers began to be arrested, Babel would show concern for their outlawed wives (*stopiatnitsas*), and had one of them move in with him and Antonina: "I'll breathe more easily if she lives with us."

Milton Ehre is convinced that Babel had a program of sorts, that his existence was "guided by a strategy of survival, a way to hold on in a culture gone mad." Nathalie Babel is even more convinced that her father had a program, even if it wasn't about survival. "His life centered on writing, and it can be said without exaggeration that he sacrificed everything to his art, including his personal relationships, his family, his liberty, even his life." Hence, he had to return to the Soviet Union. "I am a Russian writer. If I didn't live with the Russian people, I would cease being a writer. I would be like a fish out of water."

But he was a fish out of water wherever he was—Paris, Moscow, even Odessa, with its fairy-tale skies. We cannot tell what was in the notebooks and manuscripts that the Cheka took from him; no one has seen them but Babel himself (and perhaps his inquisitors). Their content remains a mystery. According to Antonina Pirozhkova, the manuscripts included a book of stories that Babel was preparing for publication. "And that's what I'll call it—'New Stories.' Then we are going to get rich." There might also have been an excerpt from *Kolya Topuz*. And in a letter to Lavrenti Beria, chief of the Cheka at the time of his arrest, Babel begs Beria to let him put "the manuscripts confiscated from me in order. . . . I burn with a desire to work." He mentions an essay on collectivism, notes for a book on Gorky, several dozen stories, a finished scenario, and a half-finished play—the "fruit" of his last eight years. Anyone with an interest in Babel has mourned this treasure trove, which disappeared when the Cheka destroyed its files in 1941, as the Germans sat outside the walls of Moscow. Legends have continued to grow about these manuscripts, that their very burning was a Stalinist ruse, that they're still sitting somewhere in the cellars of the Lubyanka. Every few years or so there's talk of an imminent Babel "sighting," of some novel that was recovered from the ashes like a priceless jewel and is on the verge of being published in the former Soviet Union. . . .

Manuscripts don't burn, says the Devil in Bulgakov's *The Master and Margarita,* but even if Babel's unpublished manuscripts had escaped the Cheka's fire by some divine intervention or devilish trick, I still have to wonder how Babel could have published a collection of "New Stories" in Stalin's age of the New Soviet Man, unless he was Kiril Lyutov again on board the propaganda train. Babel's "plumage"—his absolute belief in the cunning twists of language—was almost an attack on Stalin himself.

He could have polished and polished with the purity of a Spinoza, but he was still in some kind of fugue state. "I'm not afraid of arrest as long as they let me keep working," Babel confides to Antonina, the same Babel who was so curious about the Cheka, who had watched men and women vanish. He was running out of masks to wear and roles to play. He'd embarked on a new family, with a new child, Lydia (born in 1937), and he arrives at the maternity hospital "carrying so many boxes of chocolate that he has to steady the top of the stack with his chin"—the comical Babel, the gallant Babel, the magnanimous writer-schlemiel who hands out chocolates to every doctor and nurse in sight. However much he loved Antonina and little Lydia, what about the family he'd left behind in Belgium and France? His distance from Makhno—and the thought that he couldn't watch her grow up into a magnificent bandit chief—must have eaten him alive, this man with a morbid sense of responsibility. Babel was his own haunted house. His existence had become a kind of *Red Cavalry*—a series of short takes with several narrators. . . .

2.

THE LAST TWO STORIES that Babel published in his lifetime—"The Trial" and "Di Grasso"—offer us a tiny window into his despair. I've already talked about Nedachin, the failed jewel thief, trapped in Stalin's circus "like an animal from another world." "The Trial" reads like a parable that's a little too opaque, but "Di Grasso" is full of sinews and flesh. Our narrator is fourteen. He works for a ticket scalper, Nick Schwarz, "a tricky customer with a permanently screwed-up eye and enormous silky handle bars." But these are hard times on Theater Lane. Chaliapin is too expensive, and so the Sicilian tragedian Di Grasso comes to Odessa with his troupe. Nick Schwarz takes one look at Di Grasso's folk drama and says, "This stuff stinks." The narrator has nothing to scalp; he can't even sell his tickets at half price.

In the first act, the daughter of a rich peasant pledges herself to a shepherd, played by Di Grasso himself. But a city slicker named Giovanni arrives in a velvet waistcoat and flirts with the maiden, while Di Grasso keeps flattening himself against walls. In the second act, she gives him back his ring. In the third act, the city slicker is at the village barber, while the shepherd stands in a far corner of the stage, as gloomy as Hamlet: "[T]hen he gave a smile, soared into the air, sailed across the stage, plunged down on Giovanni's shoulder, and having bitten through the latter's throat, began, growling and squinting, to suck blood from the wound." The curtain falls, hiding "killed and killer," and Di Grasso's folk drama is declared a masterpiece. He goes on to play Lear and Othello, and confirms the terrible truth "that there is more justice in outbursts of noble passion than in all the joyless rules that run the world."

And here Babel, with his usual mischief, is poking fun at the deadening art of socialist realism. Di Grasso's troupe could be likened to Stalin's own troupe of Soviet writers. Di Grasso is as much of a swindler as Nick Schwarz—his troupe has no talent at all, and it's only through one magical leap that he blinds his audience to the mediocrity of "performance" in Stalin's little state.

In the "terrifying and playful labyrinth of Babel's fiction," nothing is what it seems—opposites attract and collide, and in that collision produce a strange motif. Di Grasso is as nonverbal as the Boss, who could barely recite his own speeches, who would sit in silence for hours and draw wolves on the back of an envelope, but with his murderous jump into the air Di Grasso is transformed into a tragedian who can mouth the Boss's favorite character, King Lear. According to one Moscow legend, the Yiddish actor Solomon Mikhoels, a close friend of Babel's and founder of the State Jewish Theater in Moscow, would come to the Kremlin in the middle of the night and sing Lear's lines for Stalin, who would always cry during the performance. But this proximity to the Boss couldn't save Mikhoels. Perhaps Stalin was secretly enraged that another man had seen him cry. He would have Mikhoels murdered in 1948. It was the Cheka that staged Mikhoels' death, having a "drunken driver" run him over in a Cheka truck. . . .

But Babel's art moves in all directions at once. Even if he's parodying the idea that Di Grasso's "outburst of noble passion" (a complete fraud) can bring justice to a joyless world, the leap itself is like an act of faith: the artist has to jump into the void, can only create by flinging himself through the barriers of language into the lyricism of "an unknown tongue."

And then there's the misadventures of the narrator in "Di Grasso." He's had to hock his father's watch to Nick Schwarz. But Nick refuses to give back this "golden turnip." And the boy, fearful of his father's wrath, decides to run away to Constantinople. For the last time, he watches Di Grasso play that shepherd "who is swung aloft by an incomprehensible power." Nick Schwarz has brought his missus to the play, a mountainous woman who looks like a grenadier with shoulders "stretching right out to the steppes."

Nick is scared of his missus, who cries after Di Grasso sucks the blood out of Giovanni. "Now you see what love means," she says to Nick. Madame sees the boy sob. She obliges Nick to return the golden turnip. "What can I expect but beastliness today and beastliness tomorrow?" she asks as she turns the corner into Pushkin Street with Nick. The boy stands there all alone, watch in hand. And he has one of those epiphanies that often frame Babel's stories, for better or worse. He has a clarity, a certain distinctness of vision, with the bronze head of Pushkin's statue "touched by the dim gleam of the moon." And for the first time he sees the things surrounding him "as they really were: frozen in silence and ineffably beautiful."

But the boy's epiphany ricochets back to Babel in a manner it had never done before. Even with his father's watch, the boy isn't free. His only freedom is Di Grasso's crazy leap, as genuine *and* fraudulent as any art; and without it, he's stuck in a glimmering world that's frozen and beautiful in its silence, as if Babel were fantasizing the "epiphany" of his own death—a landscape without him.

3.

"AFTER SLAPPING ALEXEI TOLSTOY in the face, M. returned immediately to Moscow." Thus begins Nadezhda Mandelstam's own journey with her husband, Osip, through Stalin's endless gulag, in *Hope Against Hope*. We never learn why Alexei Tolstoy, "The Red Count," got slapped. That's one of the beauties of Nadezhda's book. But the energy of that slap carries us right across Stalin's gulag with Nadezhda and Osip Mandelstam. And one can only wish that Antonina Pirozhkova had written about Babel with the same acumen and sense of impassioned detail. Why did she have to protect him so much? Nadezhda reveals all of Osip's faults—his paranoia; his need to wound himself—and he comes alive on the page as Babel never does in Pirozhkova's memoir. It's partly because Nadezhda was involved in Mandelstam's writing, had memorized every poem and could recite them like songs in her head. And Antonina was an engineer who abandoned Babel to the mystery of his own work. . . .

But we discover more from *Hope Against Hope* about Babel's time and the panic that must have paralyzed him than we ever do from any Soviet celebration of Babel. "Terror," she tells us, "was planned, like the economy, and quotas for life and death were manipulated at will." But it wasn't out of Stalin's own whim or perversity. "M. always said that they always knew what they were doing: the aim was to destroy not only people, but the intellect itself."

And with the intellect, imagination and memory. Mikhoels,

Stalin's personal King Lear, was so full of sorrow after his first wife died, he couldn't function. "He can't forget her: he goes into the closet and kisses her dresses," according to Pirozhkova. But Mikhoels' obsessive grief—his memory—had little room in Stalin's brave new world of Young Pioneers, Party apparatchiks, and shock troops.

And Nadezhda wonders why there was no rebellion among the *intelligentishki,* or anyone else who surrendered to the secret police. "We were all the same: either sheep who went willingly to the slaughter, or respectful assistants to the executioner. . . . Why did we never try to jump out of windows or give way to unreasoning fear and just run for it—to the forests, the provinces, or simply into a hail of bullets? Why did we stand so meekly as they went through our belongings?" There was "a paralyzing sense of one's own helplessness to which we were all prey, not only those who were killed, but the killers themselves. . . ."

Every single soul was marked. During one year alone, 1937, the heart of the Yezhovshchina, "Yezhov's Time," when Nikolai Yezhov ruled as chief of the Cheka, five percent of the population was arrested. Stalin's "Devil Dwarf" (*Chyortovski karlik*) would have wiped out the entire country if he'd continued at such a pace. He was gathering files on *everyone,* even the Boss and his Politburo. As one of his superiors said about him when he was a deputy sleuth: Yezhov doesn't know how to stop. But he was only Stalin's apparatchik. He did the Boss's bidding. On one particular day of the Yezhovshchina, December 12, 1937, Stalin and his lackey Molotov examined the death list that Yezhov had prepared, checked off 3,167 names, and went to the movies—perhaps to watch an American film with Shirley Temple, the Boss's favorite forbidden actress. . . .

Mandelstam, like almost everyone else, was "morbidly curious about the recluse in the Kremlin." And he would often ask himself: "Why is it that when I think of *him,* I see heads, mountains of heads? [. . .] What is he doing with all those heads?" And how could Babel, the Headless Man, or Nadezhda, or Mikhoels and Mandelstam, or Gorky himself, hope to survive near a man with a mountain of heads? Gorky would be the first to die (in 1936), probably poisoned by Genrikh Yagoda, chief of the Cheka before Yezhov and the Yezhovshchina. Stalin had lured Gorky back to the Soviet Union from Sorrento. The Boss couldn't bear to have Russia's most celebrated writer in exile. "Gorky's a proud man, and we have to bind him to the Party with strong ropes." Gorky became Stalin's prisoner, with a mansion in Moscow, two or three dachas, and an army of servants (all Cheka recruits) that kept him in a kind of golden cage.

Mandelstam would die in some transit camp two years after Gorky. He refused to eat, fearing that the other prisoners wanted to poison him—which wasn't so insane, since Stalin poisoned a lot of people. It was the *urkas,* hardened criminals, and not the political prisoners, who kept Mandelstam alive. They called him the Poet, and they fed him with their own spoons. But he didn't last out the Siberian winter. And Babel? His surveillance by the Cheka dates from 1934 when his fellow writers began to inform on him. "The writers exceed everyone else in their savagery and degradation," as Nadezhda notes. Once the hounds were upon him, it was just a matter of time. Only Nadezhda managed to escape Stalin's mountain of heads.

She was a *stopiatnitsa,* the outlaw wife of an outlaw poet. And she became a wanderer, a barefoot girl, without a fixed address. "[B]ecause I was homeless they overlooked me." Like most Russians, other than favored writers, artists, musicians, and the rest of Stalin's apparatchiks, Nadezhda was hungry half the time. "Peasants just lay quite still in their houses—exhausted from hunger. We all do this. I have spent my whole life lying down"—lying down in the dark, pretending that the Cheka didn't exist. The entire country was in an hypnotic trance. Neighbors and friends were all spies. "After 1937 people stopped meeting each other altogether." Even in the Kremlin there were no guests. Time had become a frozen wall and space "a prison ward." But there was something even more insidious. Osip's brother Evgeni believed that the real subjugation of the intelligentsia "was played not by terror or bribery [. . .] but by the word 'Revolution,' which none of them could bear to give up."

And this was Babel's downfall. He'd come riding into the Revolution on his own fanciful white horse, considered himself a cavalier who'd throw himself into the hurly-burly to write about the Red Cossacks' last stand. And however skewered his own vision had become—with Red Cossacks on the rampage, and Polish Jews stuck in the middle of some monstrous slaughter—he was still a child of the Revolution (with his own unorthodox songs). And that's why he couldn't remain in the Villa Chauvelot. This becomes clear in his speech to the first Congress of Soviet Writers, when he talked about practicing the genre of silence. The mysterious summons that brought him back from France in 1933 had come from Gorky, who wanted Babel to help him organize the congress. And Babel's speech, delivered on August 23, 1934, may have been in a "dead language," as Lionel Trilling suggests, but is still disturbing. He starts out by praising Stalin, who had called writers engineers of the human soul, more important than tanks and planes. But he talks about the birth of a revolutionary style—"the style of our period must be characterized by courage and restraint, by fire, passion, strength and joy." Of course, Babel's songs of fire had little to do with Stalin's Revolution, but so what?

He brags about the ruggedness of Soviet readers. "Now, foreign authors tell us that they search for their readers with a flashlight in broad daylight. But in our land it is the readers who march at us in closed formation. It's a real cavalry charge"—the cavalier has climbed on his white horse again.

He speaks of himself as "the past master of silence," and says that if he lived in a capitalist country, he would have "long since croaked from starvation," or been forced by his own capitalist publisher "to become a grocer's assistant."

But the silence he accuses himself of might have been just another mask. He had to project the aura of a man who was not writing, because what he did write made him the engineer of a very different kind of soul. Like Olesha, he could find no music in factories or collective farms. Olesha, according to Gleb Struve, "had the courage to say that every artist could create only within his powers. A writer can write only what he can write." And Olesha "candidly admitted that it was impossible for him to put himself into the shoes of an average workman or of a revolutionary hero, and therefore he could not write about either of them."

And Babel, who could never be direct, who gravitated toward a crooked line, wrote a few tepid tales about the *kolkhoz*, began his novel on Kolya Topuz, the Old World bandit who became a revolutionary clown, but he wasn't searching for a new style or language, as some critics suggest; he was withdrawing into the land of Benya Krik: his real electrical circuit had always been the Moldavanka, and even Lyutov, with his law degree from Petersburg, is a creature out of this dark world. The Moldavanka itself had been masked, with its dreamlike streets, and its goddess was the boy's own grandmother, who couldn't read or write Russian, who would hold books upside down, but would listen like an enraptured hawk as the boy recited his lessons—to her the music of Russian words "was sweet." She wants him to become a *bogatir*, which in her own confusion of tongues means a man who is both rich and a Herculean hero. "You must know everything," she warns him. "Everyone will fall on their knees before you and bow to you. Let them envy you. Don't believe in people. Don't have friends. Don't give them your money. Don't give them your heart" ("At Grandmother's").

And Babel did become that *bogatir*, something of a Herculean hero, who was never quite as rich as his grandmother would have liked, but who did wear the Moldavanka's masks and was quite stingy in matters of the heart. Perhaps he'd given his heart once, and only once, to Makhno. And perhaps the *bogatir* then had to flee. . . .

In 1928 Viktor Shklovsky wrote about the "Hamburg Reckoning," a system whereby the prizefighters of Hamburg would
rank themselves in individual combat without promoters, man-
agers, or the panoply of a staged fight. And I'd like to apply the
Hamburg Reckoning to Babel's supposedly lean years, in the
1930s, and examine how lean they really were.

1930

- Babel writes most of his letters to his mother and Maria
  from Moscow and his horse farm at Molodenovo. He seems
  agitated after the birth of Natasha, and scolds his mother
  about his own upbringing: "Do you chew a day-old bagel
  with seeds on it with your gums and then give it to her wet
  with saliva as you used to do to your son? [. . .] you
  rocked your son in a cradle, killing his self-reliance, and if
  the stuff I am producing turns out badly, I shall know who
  to blame." We can sense a residual jealousy: his mother has
  seen Natasha, held Natasha, and he hasn't.
- Babel works on "Gapa Guzhva," the first chapter of a novel
  about collectivization to be called *Veliknaya Krinitsa,* based
  on a Ukrainian village he'd visited in the spring. It was
  meant to herald Babel's new direction, into the heart of
  Soviet matters. And it might have worked at another
  time . . . but there was no other time. Babel's mordant peek
  at enforced collectivization from the perspective of an
  outcast whore would have been perfect for Maupassant, but
  not his Soviet son. Babel will abandon the project.
- Stalin publishes a letter in *Bolshevik* outlining the grim

future of Soviet literature: nothing should be published that does not conform to the Party's official point of view. Russian writers will become zombies with certain privileges.

- Nikolai Yezhov, the future "Iron Commissar," joins Stalin's inner circle. He's chief of the Central Committee's records department (put there by Stalin to seek out anyone who's disloyal to the Boss). This is the first important post for a man who will have a whole little bloody era named after him, the Yezhovshchina.

1931

- Babel publishes two of the best stories from the "Dovecot" cycle about his childhood—"In the Basement" (dated 1929) and "Awakening"—and "Karl-Yankel," a comic tale about a court case involving the Communist Party and the Jews of Odessa.

- He's now settled mostly in Molodenovo, thirty-five miles from Moscow: "I make my way through the snowdrifts to the stud farm, and there, under the direction of a stableman, I am learning a new profession—the handling of horses. It's a delight that isn't comparable to any other. They are prize horses, real whirlwinds." Gorky's dacha is less than a mile from Molodenovo. "They"—Stalin and his Cheka—"picked the best of places around Moscow for him." And Babel can visit him any evening, "since, for old times' sake, the rules that regulate the stream of people around him do not apply to me."

- He resumes his friendship with Evgenia Gladun, a Jewish femme fatale, almost as secretive as Babel himself. Evgenia kept a room outside Moscow where she could meet her lovers. She'd had a little fling with Babel in Berlin in 1927. But 1931 is a complicated year for the future Mrs. Nikolai Yezhov. She met Yezhov at a Black Sea resort while she was still married, and began a liaison with him, without discarding her other lovers. Yezhov will divorce his first wife to marry Evgenia. It's around this time that his new wife will begin her "soirees" in Moscow, inviting Babel, while Yezhov seethes with jealousy.

1932

- Babel publishes "The End of the Old-Folks' Home" (an Odessa tale), "Argamak," "The Road," "The S.S. *Cow-Wheat*," and "Guy de Maupassant." This can hardly be considered a fallow period.
- Nadezhda Mandelstam meets Yezhov at a government villa on the Black Sea, near "the dawn of his brief but brilliant career." She and Osip sit at the same table with the man who will become "one of the great killers of our time." He's modest and tiny—five feet tall. She remembers his limp, and the story that someone told about Yezhov's iron will as a Bolshevik: he could do the *gopak*, a Ukrainian dance with strong heel beats, "despite his game leg."
- Stalin celebrates Gorky's fortieth year as a writer: he renames cities, parks, streets, factories, collective farms, schools, and theaters throughout the Soviet Union in

Gorky's honor. The cult of Gorky is complete. Is the Boss being Machiavellian, or does he feel some strange kinship with Gorky? Both have their roots in the lower middle class—Stalin's father was a shoemaker, his mother a laundress, and all his life he would iron his own pants, mend his own shoes. Both men had to seize language for themselves, and have a maniacal reverence for the written word. Both have a habit of editing other people's work. Stalin would read books about to be published and "correct" them with his blue pencil; and Gorky would do the same for every young writer in the Soviet Union; he would also "edit" newspapers and published books, often crying over a sentence he happened to enjoy. Perhaps Stalin found in Gorky the poet he would have loved to become. Of course, that didn't prevent him from having Gorky poisoned when the Grand Old Man of Literature became a nuisance. Stalin is like Ivan the Terrible, his favorite tsar, who could kiss and kill with the same smooth gesture, and mourn those men he murdered.

- With Gorky back on Russian soil, Babel has an ally as powerful as the Soviet bureaucracy itself; in September he leaves for France.

- October 26: the Boss summons a gaggle of Soviet writers to Gorky's Moscow mansion; a meeting takes place in the absence of almost every significant writer—Akhmatova, Mandelstam, Pasternak, Bulgakov, and Babel (who's in Paris). Stalin arrives: "a small man in a dark green tunic of fine cloth, smelling of sweat and unwashed flesh." He jokes, mingles with the writers, eats and drinks in their midst. It's here that he articulates his idea about the writer's *religious* duty to the State, as an engineer of the human soul. And socialist realism is the root of this engineering. As one writer will remark: "Socialist Realism is Rembrandt, Rubens and Pepin [a Russian artist] put at the service of the working class," which means everything and nothing. "Probably no one has ever understood what exactly Socialist Realism is," writes Vitaly Shentalinsky, who pried Babel's archive from the Lubyanka and was one of the first to call the entire apparatus of Soviet writers a branch of the Cheka.

- November 8: Nadya Alliluyeva, Stalin's second wife, kills herself. The Boss had practically driven her insane, insulting her, flirting with other women. Yet he will mourn Nadya for the rest of his life. It's only after Nadya's death that he becomes the Kremlin's mad monk. Since he no longer has a wife, he will allow none of his lackeys to bring their wives to gatherings at the Kremlin or evenings at the Bolshoi. He will no longer spend his nights inside the Kremlin, though a light continues to burn in his office window: a caravan leaves the Kremlin around two in the morning and whisks him away to his sprawling dacha at Kuntsevo (a Moscow suburb), where he lives in one little room.

1933

- Gorky visits the White Sea Canal, built by convict laborers, embraces Yagoda, and starts to cry. "You rough fellows do not realize what great work you are doing!" The chief of the Cheka has become his pal. Gorky calls him Yagodka, Little Berry.

- Gorky is still free to travel outside the Soviet Union, still has his estate in Sorrento. Babel visits him there in April; he's working on a play called *Maria*, and reads portions of it to Gorky and his entourage. Set in Petersburg during the Civil War, the play includes a bunch of swindlers and war veterans without legs. Gorky is disturbed by Babel's "Baudelairean predilection for rotting meat. All the characters in your play, starting from the invalids, are putrid."

- November: Mandelstam writes his poem about Stalin; he gives us a portrait of "the Kremlin mountaineer" in sixteen lines that's more revealing than all the odes written about the Boss during his lifetime. The Boss didn't have "cockroach whiskers" *until* Mandelstam put them there.

1934

- Babel publishes "Dante Street" and "Petroleum" (about the *new* Moscow, with "trenches, pipes, and bricks everywhere . . . the stench of pitch," and smoke billowing "like at a wildfire").

Mandelstam is arrested in May. He hadn't read his poem on Stalin to more than ten people, but it created a "wildfire" all its own. Yagoda, whose literary tastes never ventured beyond *The Three Musketeers* and *The Man in the Iron Mask*, has memorized the poem, and recites it to

Stalin. The entire Cheka waits for the Boss's reaction. Stalin seems strangely passive. He's also a poet. He doesn't want Mandelstam destroyed, not yet. His edict is *Isolate but preserve.* He rings up Pasternak, chides him: "If I were a poet and my [poet] friend got into trouble I would go to any length to help him."

- May: Gorky's son Maximka dies after a lightning bout of pneumonia, probably induced by the Cheka. The way to weaken Gorky is through Maximka, "a likeable nonentity," as Gorky himself described him, loving him nonetheless, this man-boy who had nothing on his mind but racing cars and mystery novels and wanted to work for the Cheka. Gorky will never recover from Maximka's death.

- According to one of Stalin's biographers, Edvard Radzinsky, Yagoda would invite members of the Writers Union to visit his own labyrinth at the Lubyanka to "listen in" while interrogators worked on some poor *intelligentishka* until he confessed or betrayed a friend. And Babel was among the writers who "listened in."

1935
- *Maria* goes into rehearsal in Moscow but is never staged.
- Yezhov and Evgenia move from Pushkin Square to an apartment in the Kremlin; Evgenia can now hobnob with the Party elite. Her husband has become a little Red king. Yezhov's dacha in Meshchevino, with its tennis court and private movie theater, is much more palatial than Stalin's own fortress in Kuntsevo.

- Gorky tries to attend Malraux's congress in Paris (where Babel was such a hit), but Stalin won't give him a passport. The golden cage has shut around this Grand Old Man.

1936

- Babel publishes nothing of note.
- Stalin condemns Shostakovich's opera *Lady Macbeth of Mtsensk:* the music made him angry, according to Ehrenburg, and thus begins the attack on formalism— "leftist deformations, distortions." But the Grand Old Man rises up to defend *Lady Macbeth,* and the Cheka isolates him from the rest of the world, printing single copies of *Pravda* for him with all the news taken out.
- June 18: Gorky dies. He'd become dangerous to Stalin, who is purging the Party. The Boss will have the whole country mourn, but it's another one of the tricks he's learned from Ivan the Terrible—cry and cry and remain glad in your heart. And Babel realizes his own predicament in a world without Maxim Gorky: "Now they are not going to let me live."
- Yezhova, editor in chief of *SSSR v Stroike* (*Russia in Construction*), welcomes Babel onto the staff; they haven't been lovers for a long time, but that doesn't stop Yezhov from having jealous rages about Babel.
- Once Yagoda gets rid of everyone around Gorky, Stalin gets rid of Yagoda and "crowns" Yezhov as new chief of the Cheka on September 25. Yagoda has become too close to the Bolshevik "barons" Stalin intends to destroy, buying

them American cars, finding them little ballerinas from the Bolshoi. He's not the right kind of torturer. When his thugs at the Lubyanka can't extract a confession fast enough, Stalin complains: "Is this a hotel or a prison?" But the Boss is devious, as usual. He "promotes" Yagoda, appoints him Commissar for Communications in a country that can only deliver lies.

- Yezhov arrests all those loyal to Yagoda, and the Yezhovshchina begins. He will give the Boss whatever he wants—arrest, destroy, drive people to suicide; women working at the Lubyanka are "frightened of meeting him even in the corridors." But who is this Devil Dwarf? Born on May 1, 1895, in southwest Lithuania, near the Polish border. His father, a Russian from Tula, once kept a brothel. The family moves to Petersburg in 1906. The boy is barely literate, having gone to school for one or two years at the most. An apprentice tailor and mechanic at fifteen, he has his first "liaison" with another little tailor boy. He's drafted into the tsar's army during World War I, serves behind the lines as a mechanic of sorts. Disappears and reappears as a mechanic in a railroad yard, a worker in a glass factory, a cop. His fellow workers find him with a book and begin to call him Kolka Knizhnik, Nick the Bookworm. In 1919 he enlists in the Red Army, serves at a radio base in Saratov, soon becomes political commissar of the entire base; by 1936 he's Stalin's favorite apparatchik, photographed with him near some canal built by convicts under his control, wearing the same uniform as Stalin, the

same military cap, one hand thrust inside his coat, just like
the Boss. The Devil Dwarf has an angelic face and a child's
voice; he loves to sing and dance (with his lame leg). Being
Stalin's bloodhound begins to agitate him, darken his
nature: the angelic face turns black; his teeth start to fall
out; he suffers from neurasthenia (like Babel). Yezhova has
to end her Moscow "soirees." He torments her, has her
followed. She scribbles a note to him: "Kolya darling, I
earnestly beg you to check up on my whole life, everything
about me."

- Yezhov learns from Stalin, begins to edit manuscripts. He
"sculpts" Boris Pilnyak's new novel, *The Volga Flows into
the Caspian Sea,* though he himself has trouble finishing a
sentence. Pilnyak grows profoundly depressed. "There
isn't a single thinking adult in this country who hasn't
thought that he might get shot." Despite having Yezhov as
an editor, he will be arrested in 1937, shot in 1938.

- Yezhov uncovers the "Center of Centers," a web of spies
"in all spheres of Soviet life," bent on murdering Stalin (this
fanciful web is probably Stalin's own creation).

1937

- Babel is suddenly "productive" again. He publishes
"Sulak" (a tale of the Civil War), "Di Grasso," and "The
Kiss," a kind of coda to *Red Cavalry.* Lyutov is now an
officer with his own orderly, Mishka, "a cunning Cossack."
Mishka becomes his pimp, landing Lyutov a young widow
who offers him nothing less than "an increasingly violent,

never-ending, silent kiss" while he entertains her with stories of a Moscow "in which the future is raging." He becomes "betrothed" to the widow, but as is usual with Lyutov, he leaves her flat and crosses with his brigade into the borderless kingdom of Poland. Yet it's "Di Grasso" that intrigues me—it's a perfect tale for the Yezhovshchina. Di Grasso's leap could also be the savage, mindless, and bloody art of our Devil Dwarf.

- March 5: Babel's been hiding like a ghost in Gorky's dacha outside Moscow. "The house is empty but from time to time I get the impression that the shade of its departed master is lurking around." He must have realized that Gorky was communing with him ghost to ghost. "Again and again it is demonstrated to me that I cannot work if I live in Moscow." But how can anyone work in the middle of the Yezhovshchina?

- Yezhov's new title is Commissar-General of State Security, making him a Soviet marshal. He brags that he can arrest the entire Politburo if he wants to do so. He's the one man in the country who has Stalin's ear. Stalin locks himself up for hours with the Devil Dwarf, calls him Yezhevichka, Little Blackberry Bush. The Boss celebrates Yezhov the way he'd celebrated Gorky—has bridges, steamers, factories, collective farms, soccer fields, asylums, orphanages, and Cheka schools named after him. Yezhov is on everyone's lips. He's drunk half the time, debauched, sleeps with Zinaida Glikina (his wife's best friend) *and* with Zinaida's husband. He arrives at the Lubyanka in a drunken stupor, beats up prisoners during interrogations, walks around with blood on his tunic.

- Poems are written about Yezhov, who's likened to a snow leopard.

- April 3: Yagoda is arrested, and Stalin continues his little game of musical chairs, offering Yagoda's dacha to Molotov. Yagoda sits in a solitary cell in the Lubyanka; he can't eat or sleep; often he whispers to himself that God has to exist: *only* God could punish him for his loyal service to the Boss. Stalin lets him linger until 1938 and has him shot after staging a series of show trials that turn the Party into a band of terrified mice.

- Not even Budenny, Stalin's favorite warrior (and Babel's nemesis), is spared. In July, the Devil Dwarf tells Marshal Budenny that his wife, "the beautiful Mikhailova," a singer at the Bolshoi, is facing arrest. She's accused of having visited foreign embassies with the intent of becoming a spy—a tale that Yezhov himself probably invented. But the hero of the former Red Cavalry knows what to do. He escorts Mikhailova to the Lubyanka, wearing all his medals, and doesn't see her again until after Stalin's death, when he petitions the public prosecutor's office in her behalf. Mikhailova is returned to him, like some princess out of a poisoned fairy tale. She tells him how she'd been subjected to gang rape in the gulag. Budenny doesn't believe her. He calls her crazy in the head.

- September 28: Babel gives an interview at the Writers Union that's like a performance out of Kafka. It's Yezhov's time, "and the slightest indiscretion could be fatal. But it was just as dangerous to refuse an interview as to give one." When asked about his ideal audience, he says: "I aim at a reader who is intelligent, educated, and has good, exacting taste. Generally speaking, I feel that a short story can be read properly only by a very intelligent woman—the better specimens of this half of the human race sometimes have absolute taste, as some people have absolute pitch." Babel is performing his circus tricks, to ridicule without being noticed, to speak nonsense that has a glimmer of truth. There's no room for Babel or any of his readers in Stalin's private circus of women with absolute pitch—i.e., the fools and ideologues of socialist realism.

1938

- Babel publishes "The Trial."
- In October, Yezhova enters a sanitarium near Moscow, suffering from a mild nervous condition. She's thirty-four years old. In a month she will be dead. She might have been driven to suicide . . . or poisoned by the Dwarf. She writes to Stalin before she dies: "I feel like a living corpse." Yezhov does not attend her funeral.
- The Devil Dwarf is dismissed. Beria will replace him as chief of the Cheka.

1939

- Babel, who has been defending Maupassant all his life, says in one of his last conversations with Antonina: "Everything that Maupassant did came out fine, but he lacked heart." Antonina believes that Babel "had sensed a streak of terrifying loneliness and isolation in Maupassant"—his own loneliness and isolation. And perhaps like Maupassant, he also "lacked heart" in the end and could no longer escape into those webs of *nothingness* he'd spun as a writer.

- April 10: Yezhov is imprisoned in the Lubyanka; he will sit without a word and fly paper airplanes across his cell.

- May 11: Yezhov gives his wife (already dead) and Babel (still alive) the ultimate kiss of death: he accuses her and him of being spies.

- May 15. Babel is arrested *four* days after Yezhov's kiss. He says to Antonina: "They didn't let me finish," meaning his "fugitive" collection of new stories. On the way to Moscow, in the Cheka's own car, Babel says: "The worst part of this is that my mother won't be getting my letters." He's whisked right through the gates of the Lubyanka. So many myths have been engendered around this very moment. According to the daughter "of an important Chekist," Babel "seriously wounded" one of the men who wanted to arrest him. Others insist that guards saluted Babel while he was being led into the Lubyanka, and that he wore a smile on his face.

- Put on the "conveyor belt"—different teams interrogate him continuously—Babel confesses to having been part of a plot to murder the Boss. Yezhova was the ringleader of a band that includes Olesha, Eisenstein, Ehrenburg, Mikhoels, a polar explorer, and Isaac Babel. His French "handler" is André Malraux, who recruited him in 1933 to spy for France; Babel has managed to steal some mysterious secret about aerodromes and crops in the Ukraine.

- Was he completing the Cheka's own lunatic script, or was his "confession" much more original, something Babelesque, his own final fiction? *Red Cavalry* in the Lubyanka. Babel's interrogators are mostly illiterate and have not bothered to sample a single page of his. He's entered into a heart of darkness where nothing makes sense. He's Isaac Babel, after all, a fallen cavalier, the man of many masks. Hadn't Ehrenburg called him "the wise rabbi"? Wise or not, he's still a rabbi of the written word. And his captors have no language other than banalities. They're bandits who beat him with the sawed-off legs of a chair. They can coax him into admitting all kinds of conspiracies—the idea of an "aerodrome" comes from a scenario Babel has been working on. But they aren't imaginative enough to play with Babel, and Babel is obliged to play with them. In the notes he's prepared for his inquisitors, he reveals the advice he gave to filmmakers and fellow writers. "I told them [. . .] about the necessity for working to deepen their artistic individuality, no matter whether somebody needed it or not." (The Boss's cockroach whiskers would have begun to burn over that.) "If you are fundamentally flawed, then perfect this flaw in yourself and raise it to the level of art." And Babel did exactly that with his interrogators. If Yezhov has unmasked him as a "saboteur" and a spy, then Babel will create the scenario of a spy, with multiple adventures in Moscow and Paris. If Malraux had his own fighter squadron during the Spanish Civil War, then Babel will embroider tales of paratroopers and aircraft designers. If Yezhova recruited him at one of her parties, then he will invent a "harem" of spies around her. But at some point the game will have to end. Babel has incriminated his own friends, after all. When he tries to recant, no one listens. He has to humble himself to the new chief of the Cheka. "Salvation came to me in prison [. . .] in my solitude I could see the Soviet land with new eyes as she is in reality, indescribably beautiful." Beria couldn't care less about Babel's "salvation." Babel is already one of the damned. The Cheka is waiting on orders from Stalin whether to kill him or not.

1940

- January 26: Babel's "trial" takes place in Beria's own office at Butyrki Prison, since Beria himself sleeps during the day and only works at night; the "trial" lasts twenty minutes. The judges withdraw and don't even bother to deliberate: the verdict was prepared long before this little danse macabre. Babel is declared an agent of the French and Austrian intelligence services, "linked to the wife of the enemy of the people Yezhov," and the court sentences him to death.
- January 27, 1:30 A.M.: he's the first to be shot on a list of sixteen names. His body is taken to the crematorium at the

Donskoi Monastery in the middle of Moscow, his ashes
tossed into "bottomless grave number 1."

- February 4: Yezhov is shot, but not before he makes a last
request: "Tell Stalin that I shall die with his name on my
lips." His ashes will be tossed into Babel's bottomless
grave. And the master's own fiction seems to rise right out
of Donskoi and haunt this boneyard: Yezhova's tombstone
is twenty steps from grave number 1. "Even in death she is
here, next to Babel and Yezhov." Yezhova, née Feigenberg,
was born in Gomel, the second city of Belorusse, with a
Jewish population as dominant as Odessa's. And perhaps
she'd been shaped and inspired by a Moldavanka of her
own. Whatever her feelings about Babel, however much she
treasured him and the "softness" of his savage tales, she was
the one who had him near, in her own little measure of
eternity.

1941

- October 7: The Germans gather outside the gates of
Moscow, like jackals in armor. The Lubyanka is shooting
prisoners and burning its files (together with Babel's
manuscripts), as the Soviets prepare to abandon the capital.
The Boss sits in the Kremlin, puffing on his Dunhill pipe,
his papers already packed. And then, like some mad
prophet, Stalin decides not to surrender Moscow; outside,
the first snow of the season begins to fall. The Germans
have been advancing too quickly and haven't bothered to
bring their winter uniforms.

- It's November. While German planes roar overhead, Stalin decides to have his troops parade right near the enemy's lines. He has a field hospital built on the spot, should the Germans bomb *his* parade. He picks Marshal Budenny to inspect the troops. Budenny has grown fat since his days with the Red Cavalry. The parading troops assemble at Red Square. It's five o'clock in the morning. Specks of light appear on the Kremlin walls. A fierce snow begins to fall, blanketing the troops, rendering them invisible. And Budenny, on his white horse, rides out from the Kremlin gate, finds Stalin's phantom troops, and leads the parade. . . .

ISAAC BABEL WITH MAKHNO, CIRCA 1932

BABEL'S BRIDE: A LAST LOOK

1.

I N BABEL'S *COMPLETE WORKS*, on page 1025, the reader will fall upon a photograph of "Makhno" and the master in Paris, circa 1932. There's no question of pedigree—father and daughter have the same face, the same frown, the same gentle surliness, the same truculence against the world, as if they composed a colossal band of two, complete as Makhno's guerrillas or the Red Cavalry. Babel is wearing a homburg of sorts, glasses glued to his nose; Nathalie has some kind of cloche, white gloves, white socks, white shoes, and a little coat with a cape. She's sitting on the fence of a garden or square, with Babel holding her, while she's holding what looks like a checkered bag. . . .

It was this melodic line that I wanted to revive when I went looking for Makhno in Washington, D.C. I was like some crazy picador preparing to prod Nathalie's memory, obliging her to be little Natasha again, posing with her dad, to recall the frowns below the tilted line of her cloche. I expected something miraculous from Makhno, so that I could describe that tiny guerrilla waltzing with the master in some public garden. She was barely three when Babel arrived like a Russian Yankee Doodle prepared to conquer Paris. She remembered *nothing* at all. I panicked. I begged for one little detail, a ghostly remembrance spun out of some magic tissue of the past. But I wasn't dealing with a sentimental idiot. She still had the frown that Babel would wear his entire life—that mark of the born intelligence man. And why the hell was I so severe? I couldn't summon up a single memory from the time I was three. It would be no different if Isaac Babel had been my dad. . . .

All right, I'd accept a short novel from Nathalie about Babel's final trip to Paris, a Proustian feast with madeleines and all, something I could dip into the tea that Nathalie served in Russian cups. But there were no madeleines in her memory; Babel only danced around a bit like the ghost that he was, danced in and out of Nathalie's dreams. It was 1935. "I remember the excitement of my mother, how agitated she was. She was telling me a lot about it [her father's imminent arrival]. I was both shy and aggressive. . . . I had never seen a man in my mother's bed. [Of] that I have an image quite clear."

And she recalled Babel's departure through the prism of her mother. "As excited and happy as she was before, she was very downcast after [he left]." I probed and probed like a picador, and Makhno came up with one more memory. "My mother is at the sink, in our apartment, my father is sitting at the table with me. All of a sudden she starts to cry. The knife she was using went through her hand. She was opening oysters. I remember him jumping, grabbing her arm. I must have been very shocked. . . . I remember her with a bandaged hand. That moment when she cried and he jumped. I was petrified."

And Nathalie played with her own reminiscences. "Why was *she* opening the oysters? She probably assumed all the household functions. She did all the shlepping."

Nathalie could not recollect any other man in her mother's bed. "She spoke about him all my life." Nathalie kept asking: "Why isn't my father with us?" And Zhenya's usual answer: he couldn't leave Russia and his writing. It must have angered such a little girl: *Issya was too busy with his writing to be with her.* And she would resist her father's writing for a long, long time. After she arrived in America (to teach French at Barnard in 1961), and Babel had become a magical name in New York, a man happened to stare at her during a dinner party and say, " 'I'm sitting next to an historical monument.' It was one of the things that hurt me. I didn't want to hear about my father. I was rebelling."

And Nathalie recalled the saddest day in her mother's life. It was in the summer of 1940. "She burned Isaac's letters as the Germans were crossing the Maginot line. She knew what revolution and occupation meant" and what the Germans might do to Nathalie if they ever found Babel's letters, the same Babel whose books had been burnt by Nazis in Berlin. "We lived in a *pavillon*, a little house [with a fireplace in one of the rooms]. I walked into the room and saw my mother crying and feeding the letters into the fireplace. I stood rooted to the ground. I knew something important was happening. That was imprinted in my brain. I remember the position of the fireplace in the room. I remember the drops of water on the windowpanes [in the summer heat]."

In 1941, Nathalie and her mother found themselves in the west of France, in the provincial city of Niort. And Zhenya was arrested a few months before Nathalie's twelfth birthday. The local French police had rounded up all the Russian women in Niort (a dozen or so) and deposited them in the local jail, since Russians in occupied France were considered "politically dangerous" after the collapse of the Molotov-Ribbentrop Pact. The other women were freed, but not Zhenya—the wife of a celebrated Soviet writer who was also a *youpin,* a Yid. Nathalie could talk to her mother only across a ditch. "If you don't get me out right away, I will perish," Zhenya said to her daughter in Russian, her words floating across a ditch that belonged in a surreal movie set.

Nathalie's life had become surreal. She was also alone. She went to the mayor, she went to the police. No one could help her. Finally she went to the German Kommandant of Niort, who was married to an Englishwoman and was himself of French ancestry. The Kommandant welcomed Nathalie into his office, dismissed his only aide, and had a tête-à-tête with his little petitioner, who had all the pluck in the world. "I told him that my mother was innocent, that I had no one else, and that he had to let her go."

Zhenya was released in two days, and mother and daughter spent four years in Niort like a pair of lost birds. "We were homeless, penniless, and displaced." Nathalie never went back to Niort. "It has remained for me a place out of time, out of space, out of tangible reality." Yet without her realizing it, Niort would give Nathalie a certain strength—it was a kind of *zero degree* where all writers start, an undressed landscape where she could not pretend to hide, a black well that would free her to write about her father and herself, a reverse Moldavanka, a strange dark void where the imagination sometimes dwells. . . .

2.

I WAS ATTACHED to Zhenya, felt she had formed Babel in some crucial way, spent her whole life mourning a husband she had lost to another country (Soviet Russia), to another woman (first Tamara and then Antonina), and to the hidden language of his own craft. Nathalie had given interview after interview, but nobody had bothered to ask about her mother. "To me she belongs to that generation of people who came just before or after the Revolution and whose life was a tragedy. . . . My feelings for my mother are overshadowed by her death. Her death is devastating to me. I mourned for years. Her influence was very strong, even after she was gone."

I wanted to know what she was like, to feel her through Natasha's eyes. "Her friends called her Countess—my mother was extremely dignified. She obviously had a great appeal to people. She was also very intransigent, moralistic, probably a little prudish. But when I was eighteen, nineteen, twenty, I was jealous [of her]." The boys Nathalie brought home "were quickly more interested in my mother than in me."

But she'd come to Paris in 1925 as a painter, and I didn't hear one peep about her paintings—we have photos of Zhenya and Babel at a beach in Belgium, photos of Babel and Maria, who's wearing a white cloche, photos of Babel at Molodenovo, with a beautiful black horse behind him, but not one image of Zhenya's art. "She never had enough money to buy paint." Much of Zhenya's work was lost when she and Nathalie had to leave their *pavillon* in Plessis Robinson (a suburb south of Paris), and move to Niort, but Nathalie did have a painting and a drawing that her mother had done after the war. The drawing was of Nathalie's first love, a boy named Emmanuel, who was seven or eight years older than she. I smiled my own novelist's smile—Nathalie, hiding from a father who had hid himself from her, had chosen as her first love a boy with her father's patronymic (Emmanuelovich). "She [Zhenya] and Emmanuel had a very nice relation, except when it came to sex" (that is, Nathalie's own sexuality). But the portrait of Emmanuel startled me. He had a delicate, androgynous face, with a curl over one eye. And I wondered if Zhenya had softened his features on purpose, to minimize him in a magical way, remove any male hook he might have had. . . .

The painting was even more mysterious. It was the portrait of a woman and child, done before the war. The woman's eyes are nearly closed; the child is wearing a red scarf, leaning against the woman; both have brown hair; we can see only one of the child's eyes. The sex of the child is vague—could be a boy or a girl. The child seems troubled; the woman has a hand near her heart. The background is blue-white, but the painting has its own treasure—a secret painting on its backside, a pentimento from an earlier period. It looks like a Russian village. Was it a glimpse of Zhenya's own childhood in the Ukraine? Nathalie didn't have a clue. . . .

We got onto the subject of Ilya Ehrenburg, who had been courageous in resurrecting Babel's work during the 1950s, when Babel was still a no-no of Russian literature. Ehrenburg's own career was deeply ambiguous. He'd survived the Yezhovshchina and Stalin's other purges, and should have been shot for having lived among foreigners so long—Stalin distrusted *anyone* who'd been abroad, even prisoners of war—but Ilya would become the Boss's favorite columnist during World War II, and his dispatches about the fall of France put Soviet readers under his spell. Ehrenburg had walked a much simpler tightrope than Isaac Babel. Or as Vasily Shentalinsky says: "He was a clever performer" who managed to "outlive all his friends." He was *Izvestia*'s man in Paris, its window onto the West, and could champion writers such as Hemingway and Malraux without threat of punishment. He was a kind of court jester who considered himself "Cultural Ambassador of the Soviet Union." And as Babel observed to his inquisitors at the Lubyanka: "Soviet writers when they arrived in Paris always visited Ehrenburg first of all. Acquainting them with the city, he would 'instruct' them as he thought best," like a handmaiden . . . or a watchdog.

But he was always devoted to Babel, loved his idiosyncrasies: "It was not only in his appearance that Babel was unlike a writer, he also lived differently. He did not have mahogany furniture, or bookcases, or a secretaire. He even did without a desk and wrote on a kitchen table; at Molodenovo, where he rented a room with the village cobbler Ivan Karpovich, he used a joiner's bench."

Once, during the Yezhovshchina, while they were sitting in the restaurant of Moscow's Metropole Hotel, with the band playing and dancers swirling near the tables, Babel leaned over to him and whispered: "Yezhov is only the instrument." And Ehrenburg, like everyone else in the Soviet Union, shivered inside his pants. But perhaps he had a little less to shiver about. His own writing never lived near the razor's edge. He wasn't capable of cutting through the bone, like Babel could. His whole oeuvre was one vast straight line with a couple of bumps. . . .

But Ilya himself was much more complex. He was a Nabokovian character who positioned himself between Isaac and Zhenya and played out his own curious dance. In 1946, while still living in Niort, Zhenya was summoned to Paris: Ilya wanted to see her. She'd known him since her early days in Paris. "When my mother arrived, she lived in a hotel where there were many Russians. Ehrenburg lived in the same hotel." Nathalie believes that Ehrenburg tried to sleep with her. "Mother wasn't delicate in turning him down. She probably hurt his feelings—he never forgave her." And from that point on "they obviously hated each other." But she met with Ehrenburg. And this is when he began to sin against Zhenya and Babel himself. He told her that Babel was still alive, that he'd spent the war in exile "and was now living under surveillance not far from Moscow."

Who had instructed him to deliver such a monstrous lie? Was it his Soviet handlers, or the Boss himself? Stalin was always meddling, and the Boss couldn't afford to appear as the executioner of Isaac Babel, one of the rare Soviet writers with a readership in the West. And let's suppose that Ehrenburg was also duped, that he was as blind as his own message, but did he really believe that Babel, or his ghost, was coming back?

Ilya wasn't the only messenger. Total strangers began to stop Zhenya in the street, tell her tales about Babel's life in some Siberian prison. Zhenya soon realized that there was nothing random about these little strangers, who were probably "Soviet plants."

Zhenya would meet with Ehrenburg again, in 1956, while she herself was quite ill, suffering from cancer. Ilya told her that Babel had been "rehabilitated," that he was no longer an enemy of the people, that he could be read in the Soviet Union, that his name would miraculously reappear in encyclopedias and schoolbooks; Ilya wanted Zhenya to sign a paper certifying that she and Babel "had been divorced since before the war." Whose agent was he this time? The Boss was already dead. And Ilya knew that Zhenya and Isaac had never been divorced. He then told her that Babel had a "second wife" and a daughter.

Zhenya asked for the name of this child, and Ehrenburg answered with incredible cruelty: "Natasha." He meant to wound her, make her feel that Babel had duplicated *her* life with another woman, giving him two daughters with an identical name, as if to rob Zhenya of her own existence. Nathalie is kind enough to consider that Ehrenburg might have made a slip of the tongue. "What I do know is that my mother then spat in his face and fainted."

3.

IN THE EARLY SIXTIES, while she was in New York, Nathalie was approached by an American publisher to edit a collection of letters by Babel to his mother and sister. She was reluctant at first. But no one else could identify all the names mentioned in the letters—no one else could talk about Lyova, the lost uncle in America, or Maria's husband, or the particulars surrounding Babel's "crazy" mother-in-law. And in preparation, Nathalie began to reread all of Babel's stories; she could revisit her own childhood, when Zhenya would sing the stories to her like lullabies. It was pure romance, as if Nathalie had fallen in love with her father again, though the love had always been buried somewhere. And Makhno, the little guerrilla whom Babel had discovered in his daughter, began to devote herself to Babel and all his contradictions. "In spite of my reluctance, and even a pathological resistance, my father simply caught up with me." And she's been trying to catch up with him ever since, presenting Babel with his wonders and his warts to each new generation of American readers.

The two long essays she's written about him (from *The Lonely Years* and *The Complete Works*) are marvels of their own, love letters to Isaac (and his readers) that deepen the details of his life—Nathalie introduces Babel's own father as "a man of imposing physique and impetuous nature"—but still retain the sting of a daughter who had to travel very far to find Isaac. "Makhno" is never sentimental when she writes about Babel or herself—she has lived in silence and secrecy, like her father. And after finishing both essays, we're left with an almost magical melancholy and the feeling that in order to complete her own journey with Babel, she will have to "return" to Niort again and again, reach into that dark well somewhere in her psyche. . . .

Nathalie's own relationship with Antonina (who's still alive as I write this sentence) is even more complicated than one might think. Nathalie first met her in 1961, four years after her own mother's death. It was Lydia, her half sister, who brought Nathalie through the dark foyer and up the stairs of Babel's "last house" in Moscow. "I saw a woman on the landing. I looked at her and what came out of my mouth has never failed to astonish me. 'How you resemble my mother!' I blurted out—and then we both cried in each other's arms. I was amazed. Here was another woman who, like my mother, had never stopped loving my father, who had never wavered in her devotion to him."

But this, unfortunately, would be the highest point of an ever declining hill. Nathalie and Antonina now live a few subway stops away from each other. They seem locked in some climate of distrust that's like a Balzacian battle. It was Nathalie who helped bring Antonina, Lydia, and Lydia's son to the United States. I talk of my own meeting with Antonina and Lydia in Paris. I mention Antonina's white hair.

"Red," Nathalie says, ruining my own memories.

"The woman is hard as rock. I was accused of robbing them [Antonina and Lydia]. I was covered with insults. Our relationship ended, but they were watching me like a falcon. They sent me a certificate from the USSR. When I saw the certificate, I und everything I wanted to know" about Ehrenburg. It claimed that Antonina, as Babel's wife, "was the only heir to all his possessions and writings in the whole world." And the date on this document was three weeks after Zhenya met with Ehrenburg in 1956. "You cannot imagine the power wielded by this man. He promised Antonina that he would come back with proof of a divorce." And I tried to figure out the logic behind Ilya's legerdemain. Was he representing himself or the Soviet government in his machinations and maneuvers with Zhenya?

"Ehrenburg undoubtedly considered Antonina a more suitable widow than my mother," an émigré artist and daughter of a Jewish industrialist. Antonina had Soviet credentials that Zhenya neither had nor wanted—she was the first woman construction engineer to work on the Moscow metro; it was easier to rehabilitate Babel with Antonina along on the ride as his "legitimate wife." But however much he wanted to honor Antonina, Ilya must have known that he was dishonoring the past of a man he claimed to love and admire, turning him into a Soviet saint, with a Soviet wife and Soviet child. "He understood the Revolution and recognized it as a pledge of future happiness," Ilya wrote about Babel, the wise rabbi, as if Babel himself were just another toy of socialist realism. The wise rabbi had never really been "rehabilitated," because his writing remains problematical, with its lashing modernism that eats into the idea of any dogma or belief. Babel belongs nowhere, certainly not in the *new* Russia, which has been just as niggardly as the old about celebrating a *zhid* from Odessa who wrote about Jewish bandits and Jewish revolutionists like Gedali, "a tiny, lonely visionary in a black top hat," who dreams of "an International of good people," while Lyutov talks of blood and dreams of "a Jewish glass of tea" ("Gedali").

"Creativity does not dwell in palaces," Babel once wrote, nor does it dwell in allegiance to *anyone*—it exists outside the realm of reward. Babel went into the darkness and wrote *Red Cavalry*, and that book belongs to his readers, whoever we are. And in some profound way, it also belongs to Nathalie Babel, not because she's any more "legitimate" than Antonina or Lydia, but because she's the one who has continued his story. Antonina's claims to Babel's "possessions" might be twice as *authentic* as Nathalie's. I couldn't care less. I'm not in the business of arbitration. But if Babel was shot in the head in one of Stalin's cellars, with a little dirty towel to catch the blood, then the Boss and his henchmen had a harder time killing him than they could ever have imagined. His toughness, his singularity, is there in Makhno's face and in those sad "love letters" to all of Babel's readers that seem to come right out of the empty spaces in Niort. Nathalie is a minimalist in her own fashion, as brave as that little girl who danced in front of the Kommandant and demanded her mother's release. . . .

AFTERWARD

1.

I T WAS 1965 OR SO. I was an assistant professor at Stanford during that honeymoon period when English departments were no longer at war with living writers and welcomed them onto the campus. We were still orphans who weren't allowed to teach Dickens or James Joyce, because we didn't have a doctorate and couldn't have understood the complexities of craft, but who was I to gripe? Stanford paid my bills, supported my delusion of being a novelist. It also raised men from the dead, meaning that Alexander Fyodorovich Kerensky, the prime minister of Russia's Provisional Government in 1917 (before the Bolsheviks staged their little putsch), was going to appear at the university. I hadn't heard a peep about Kerensky since his four months in power. And here he was, almost fifty years later, as if there were some time warp, and an old minister like him could slide right out from under his little moment of glory. I remember a tall man with cropped hair—*Kerensky*. Or perhaps my own time warp has made him tall. He was introduced by Bertram Wolfe, a former radical who had turned against the Soviets and was now affiliated with Stanford's own conservative think tank, the Hoover Institution.

We were sitting in a classroom, fifty of us, students and teachers, and Bertram Wolfe talked and talked and talked. He was praising Kerensky, but it was almost like a moment out of Nabokov's *Pnin,* where the professor babbles to an empty auditorium. The students around me had to leave for their next class. Kerensky sat with a grim, gray look; Bertram Wolfe could have been another devil, like Ilyich (Vladimir Lenin). He was well into his eighties, Alexander Fyodorovich, but he hadn't given up his own lost war. He didn't have time to arrest Lenin and those other scoundrels, he told us. "I had to make sure that the trolley cars would run."

Was it the lament of a sore loser? History hasn't been kind to Alexander Fyodorovich. And I had to wonder what Russia would have been like under his much milder democracy. For the Soviets, he would become a figure of fun. Babel writes about him in an early story, "Line and Color." It's 1916. Our narrator claims to have met Kerensky at a sanitarium in Finland. "The dining-room smelled of pine trees, of the Countess Tyszkiewicz's fresh shoulders, and of the English officers' silk underwear." The countess is as beautiful as Marie Antoinette (another loser). Alexander Fyodorovich cannot distinguish her beauty. He's nearsighted. Our narrator lectures him about the magnificence of Line, that "mistress of the world," which escapes Kerensky. He sees nothing of the magic garden they are walking in, surfaces "that undulate like a line drawing by Leonardo." The narrator begs Alexander Fyodorovich to buy a pair of glasses.

But Kerensky has the better of him. He doesn't want to squander his money on spectacles. "I don't need your line, vulgar as truth is vulgar. You live your life as though you were a teacher of trigonometry, while I for my part live in a world of miracles. . . . What do I need lines for, when I have color? To me the whole universe is a gigantic theater, and I am the only member of the audience who hasn't glued opera glasses to his eyes."

The narrator departs from Finland with his tail between his legs. Six months later, he sees Kerensky again. It's June 1917, and Alexander Fyodorovich is "now supreme god of our armies and arbiter of our destinies." But his nearsightedness doesn't stand him in good stead. A bridge has been dismantled. "Streetcars lay like dead horses in the streets." A rally is held at the House of the People. Alexander Fyodorovich gives a speech about Russia, "mystic mother and spouse," while his head is deep in clouds of color. "The animal passion of the crowd stifled him." On his private planet, without opera glasses, he cannot see the growing anger of the crowd. He steps down from the podium, and it's Trotsky who climbs up after him, Trotsky who twists his mouth and barks at the audience in his merciless voice, full of line *and* color. "Comrades!"

Of course Babel has it both ways. Alexander Fyodorovich is the visionary—the artist-dreamer with his own musical spectrum of color, who believes in great bundling forms rather than fine lines, but who cannot sway an audience, cannot rule. Yet he rules "Line and Color," like a quaint and curious bomb within the Soviet canon. The story was published in 1923, but if we go back to 1918, when Babel wrote for *New Life,* Gorky's anti-Bolshevik magazine, we find him much closer to Kerensky than to Ilyich—he offers us the bitter colors of a St. Petersburg trapped in a surreal spell, where horses in a Soviet slaughter-house "stand crestfallen in stalls," "somnolent with exhaustion," chewing on their own dung, and where "soulless, stunted women" give birth to little blue monsters with silent mouths and "wide, serious eyes."

Ilyich wasn't too happy with Gorky's *New Life.* He shut it down that July (1918). But he could do nothing about Gorky himself. Gorky was much more loved than Lenin. Ilyich had met him in 1905, when Gorky was a world-famous writer *and* revolutionary, and Lenin was simply an outlaw. People wanted to touch the young god from Nizhni Novgorod. Tolstoy called him a peasant "with a pugnacious nose, Asiatic cheekbones, and a big body, all bone and muscle." Gorky had become Chekhov's protégé. "Like a rocket he flew from nowhere into our quiet intelligentsia life," said Olga Knipper, Chekhov's actress wife. The police followed him everywhere. He was kicked out of Nizhni. The tsar's henchmen would have him arrested, and Tolstoy would get him out of jail. He moved to Petersburg and was thrown into the Peter and Paul Fortress, where he might have rotted forever, but his popularity was too great, even for Peter and Paul. Thousands in Western Europe began to protest, and Gorky was "invited" to vacate the tsar's little empire. He settled in Capri, where Lenin visited him in 1910. They went fishing together like two barefoot boys. Gorky was attracted to men without scruples who wanted to win at any price—*ozorniki*, like Ilyich. Gorky set up his own "court of Russian art and letters" on Capri. It almost seemed as if literature itself was in exile with Gorky. He'd become the moral heart of Russia, even while he was in the West. . . .

He sailed back to Petersburg in 1913, founded the magazine *Letopis*, without which Babel and a host of other writers might never have been published. Gorky's Petersburg apartment was like a hotel for starving writers. He would often cry in the middle of reading a manuscript. "It is to books that I owe everything that is good in me." He would carry Russian literature around with him on his back, before, after, and during the Revolution. Trotsky, who never liked him, called Gorky "culture's psalm-singer." But Gorky understood the ravages that the Revolution would bring. It was Zinoviev, one of the Revolution's main "architects," who boasted: "The bourgeoisie kill separate individuals; but we kill whole classes." He could have been talking about Stalin, Trotsky . . . or Ilyich. Intellectuals were not the country's brains "but its excrement," according to Ilyich. And long before Stalin, he started his own Red Terror. He got rid of the tsar's secret police and organized the Cheka, sometimes with the same policemen. He pecked whole pieces out of the intelligentsia. But Gorky stood in his way. Gorky put aside his own writing and saved as many artists and intellectuals as he could. His apartment became a hospital and a house of culture. He would hide some grand duke, guard him with a bulldog wrapped in a blanket so that the dog "would not bite proletarian visitors." He began to accumulate wives, sisters, and sons—adopting every lost soul who came to him.

No one but Gorky could stand up to Lenin. "There is something frightening about the sight of this great man, who pulls the levers of history on our planet as he wishes." Gorky petitioned him about a young sailor who was going to be shot. Ilyich grumbled. "Alexey Maximovich, for God's sake—don't come to me with all these trifles. Don't you understand—this is *one* boy. There's a revolution going on." But the sailor was saved.

Ilyich kept hinting that Gorky go somewhere on a *permanent* vacation. The barefoot boy went into exile again. And some critics can't seem to comprehend his fondness for Stalin. He could have been "dining on diamonds" if he'd "submitted" to Ilyich. Then why did he allow Stalin to seduce him? Even if Stalin's flattery made him feel like "Mary Pickford," he was already a star without one of Stalin's jubilees. But Gorky was comfortable around the Boss. Stalin wasn't the son of a school official, like Ilyich. Stalin never studied law in Kazan and Petersburg. Gorky was blind to the Boss's murderous nature. At least until the end of his life. "We are engaged in trifles and now the very stones in our country are singing," he babbled just before he died. The last note he dictated was "End of novel, end of hero, end of author."

2.

BABEL NEVER HAD a chance. A *zhid* from Odessa who flourished for a little while, thanks to Gorky. But Gorky could have "fathered" him forever and still wouldn't understand his writing: "His laconism is a double-edged quality; it can teach or kill Babel." It wasn't Babel's shorthand that killed him, savage or not. It was the deadening saga of Stalin's machine. Yet it's curious. Sixty years after the master's own demise in a Cheka killing room we have another Benya Krik. He also sits in prison. He was arrested on October 25, 2003. State security men in masks grabbed him off his private jet while it was refueling somewhere in Siberia; they were part of Vladimir Putin's own Cheka. Putin himself had been a Cheka chief before Boris Yeltsin handpicked him as president. But there was trouble inside the Kremlin's walls. It had become a divided house, composed of "the family," officials who favored free enterprise, and the *siloviki* (strongmen), army generals and Putin's old lieutenants from the Cheka. The *siloviki* seemed to win. They were frightened of Benya Krik—otherwise known as Mikhail Khodorkovsky, Russia's richest man. Like Benya, Mikhail had a "Jewish background." But he didn't come from Odessa, which has fallen off the map. He was born in Moscow, in 1963. Both his parents were factory workers, and Mikhail was raised in a communal apartment. He joined the Communist Party's youth league—the Komsomol— and rose within its ranks. The Party helped him go into business, rewarded him with government contracts, financed his own bank. He was part of Boris Yeltsin's coterie of businessmen; in 1993, he even served alongside the minister of energy. He would become an oil and banking baron, "the bad boy of Russian business," who locked minority shareholders out of meetings and laundered money for the Russian mafia.

It wasn't his "rough play" that bothered the Kremlin. It was his sudden interest in politics. Up until recently the Kremlin was his *krysha,* his roof of protection. But he turned away from the Kremlin. He donated a hundred thousand dollars to one of Laura Bush's favorite projects, the National Book Festival, had himself photographed with the President and the First Lady. He was Benya Krik . . . and Jay Gatsby—a man who'd come out of his own Platonic image: he challenged Putin, began financing rival candidates and parties, even imagined himself as the next Russian president.

Mikhail doesn't wear orange pants. But he has Benya's bravura. And perhaps the Cheka will destroy him as it destroyed the King. I won't predict his future. He might have become king of the Kremlin by the time you read this book. Or he might still be sitting in Moscow's Matrosskaya Tishina prison. Whatever his fate, Benya Krik is alive and well. Nothing can replace or harm him, not even masked gunmen on a Siberian airstrip. It's no wonder there's never been another story quite like "The King." Fairy tales are hard to find; Moscow may be the new Wild West, but it's not the Moldavanka, that fetid hothouse of Babel's imagination. And perhaps the rats and damp rot of Matrosskaya Tishina are as close to the Moldavanka as Mikhail will ever get. The Chekists should have known that *this* Benya might thrive in the dark, like some magnificent bulb. And at least in my own imagination, Mikhail Khodorkovsky is a sign that Babel's own work is alive and well, that it has entered our new millennium with all its plumage intact.

"After every story I age a few years," Babel would often brag, like one of his unreliable narrators. Perhaps now we can forgive him for the myths he loved to build around himself, lies about his life and his craft. Perhaps it was his own way to navigate the Soviet Union, though he should have realized it was unnavigable. The coast was never clear. He rode across the Revolution on some lyrical white horse, and finally he took a terrible fall. Perhaps he was even closer to Kerensky than he could have imagined. Perhaps Kerensky's colors burst in front of his own eyes. While Ilyich and Stalin were busy destroying people, Babel might have been thinking about trolley cars that had to move along a bumpy line, or else creativity and wonder would begin to break.

SELECTED BIBLIOGRAPHY

Arbus, Diane. *Diane Arbus.* New York: Aperture, 1972.

Avins, Carol J. Introduction to Isaac Babel, *1920 Diary.*

Babel, Isaac. *The Collected Stories.* Trans. Walter Morison. Reprint. Cleveland: Meridian Books, 1960.

——. *The Complete Works of Isaac Babel.* Ed. Nathalie Babel. Trans. Peter Constantine. New York: Norton, 2002.

——. *The Lonely Years 1925–1939.* Ed. Nathalie Babel. Trans. Andrew R. MacAndrew and Max Hayward. Reprint. Boston: David R. Godine, 1995.

——. *1920 Diary.* Ed. Carol J. Avins. Trans. H. T. Willets. New Haven: Yale University Press, 1995.

——. *You Must Know Everything: Stories 1915–1937.* Ed. Nathalie Babel. Trans. Max Hayward. Reprint. New York: Dell Publishing, 1970.

Babel, Nathalie. "Afterword: A Personal Memoir." In Isaac Babel, *The Complete Works of Isaac Babel.*

——. Introduction to Isaac Babel, *The Lonely Years.*

Barna, Yon. *Eisenstein.* Trans. Lise Hunter. Bloomington: Indiana University Press, 1973.

Barthes, Roland. *Writing Degree Zero.* Trans. Annette Lavers and Colin Smith. New York: Hill & Wang, 1968.

Bellow, Saul. "Where Do We Go from Here: The Future of Fiction." In Irving Malin, ed., *Saul Bellow and the Critics*.

Bloom, Harold, ed. *Modern Critical Views: Isaac Babel*. New York: Chelsea House, 1987.

Brown, Edward J., ed. *Major Soviet Writers: Essays in Criticism*. New York: Oxford University Press, 1973.

Burgin, Richard. *Conversations with Jorge Luis Borges*. New York: Holt, 1969.

Carden, Patricia. *The Art of Isaac Babel*. Ithaca: Cornell University Press, 1972.

Charyn, Jerome. *Hemingway: Portrait de l'artiste en guerrier blessé*. Paris: Découvertes Gallimard, 1999.

Conquest, Robert. *The Great Terror: A Reassessment*. Reprint. London: Pimlico, 1992.

Ehre, Milton. *Isaac Babel*. Boston: Twayne, 1986.

Ehrenburg, Ilya. "The Wise Rabbi." In Harold Bloom, ed., *Modern Critical Views: Isaac Babel*.

———. *Memoirs: 1921–1941*. Trans. Tatiana Shebunina. Cleveland: World Publishing, 1964.

———. "Moscow Commemoration of Babel's Seventieth Birthday." In Isaac Babel, *You Must Know Everything*.

Falen, James E. *Isaac Babel: Russian Masters of the Short Story*. Knoxville: University of Tennessee Press, 1974.

Fiedler, Leslie A. "Saul Bellow." In Irving Malin, ed., *Saul Bellow and the Critics*.

Freidin, Gregory. "Fat Tuesday in Odessa: Isaac Babel's 'Di Grasso.' " In Harold Bloom, ed., *Modern Critical Views: Isaac Babel*.

Frydman, Anne. Introduction to A. N. Pirozhkova, *At His Side*.

Gogol, Nikolai. *Dead Souls*. Trans. Bernard Guilbert Guerney. Reprint. New York: Rinehart Editions, 1948.

———. *Taras Bulba*. Trans. Peter Constantine. New York: Modern Library, 2003.

Hallett, Richard William. *Isaac Babel*. New York: Frederick Ungar, 1973.

Howe, Irving. "The Right to Write Badly." In Harold Bloom, ed., *Modern Critical Views: Isaac Babel*.

Hurlihy, Patricia. *Odessa: A History, 1794-1914.* Cambridge, Mass.: Harvard Ukrainian Research Institute, 1986.

Jansen, Marc, and Nikita Petrov. *Stalin's Loyal Executioner: People's Commissar Nikolai Ezhov.* Stanford, Calif.: Hoover Institution Press, 2002.

Levin, Dan. *Stormy Petrel: The Life and Work of Maxim Gorky.* New York: Appleton-Century, 1965.

Malin, Irving, ed. *Saul Bellow and the Critics.* New York: The Gotham Library, 1967.

Mandelstam, Nadezhda. *Hope Against Hope: A Memoir.* Trans. Max Hayward. New York: Atheneum, 1970.

Markish, Simon. "The Example of Isaac Babel." *Commentary,* November 1977.

Meyers, Jeffrey. *Hemingway: A Biography.* Reprint. New York: Perennial Library, 1986.

Munblit, Georgy. "Reminiscences of Babel." In Isaac Babel, *You Must Know Everything.*

Nikulin, Lev. "Years of Our Life: Babel on His Seventieth Birthday." In Isaac Babel, *You Must Know Everything.*

O'Connor, Frank. "The Romanticism of Violence." In *The Lonely Voice.* Cleveland: World Publishing, 1963.

Ozick, Cynthia. Introduction to Isaac Babel, *The Complete Works of Isaac Babel.*

Paley, Grace. Foreword to A. N. Pirozhkova, *At His Side.*

Paustovsky, Konstantin. *Years of Hope.* Trans. Manya Havari and Andrew Thomson. New York: Pantheon, 1968.

Pirozhkova, A. N. *At His Side: The Last Years of Isaac Babel.* Trans. Anne Frydman and Robert L. Busch. South Royalton, Vt.: Steerforth Press, 1996.

Poggioli, Renato. "Isaac Babel in Retrospect." In Harold Bloom, ed., *Modern Critical Views: Isaac Babel.*

Radzinsky, Edvard. *Stalin.* Trans. H. T. Willets. Reprint. London: Sceptre, 1997.

Rosenstone, Robert A. *King of Odessa.* Evanston, Ill.: Northwestern University Press, 2003.

Rosenthal, Raymond. "The Fate of Isaac Babel." *Commentary*, February 1947.

Seton, Maria. *Sergei M. Eisenstein.* Reprint. London: Dennis Hobson, 1978.

Shentalinsky, Vitaly. *Arrested Voices: Resurrecting the Disappeared Writers of the Soviet Union.* Trans. John Crowfoot. New York: The Free Press, 1993.

Shklovsky, Viktor. "Isaac Babel: A Critical Romance." Trans. Catherine Brown. In Harold Bloom, ed., *Modern Critical Views: Isaac Babel.*

Sinyavsky, Andrey. "Isaac Babel." Trans. Catherine Brown. In Edward J. Brown, ed., *Major Soviet Writers.*

Sontag, Susan. Preface to Roland Barthes, *Writing Degree Zero.*

Stein, Peter. "Isaac Babel and Violence." In Harold Bloom, ed., *Modern Critical Views: Isaac Babel.*

Trilling, Diana. *The Beginning of the Journey: The Marriage of Lionel and Diana Trilling.* Orlando: Harcourt Brace, 1993.

Trilling, Lionel. Introduction to Isaac Babel, *The Collected Stories of Isaac Babel.*

———. *The Liberal Imagination: Essays on Literature and Society.* Reprint. Garden City, N.Y.: Doubleday Anchor, 1957.

Wilson, Edmund. *The Wound and the Bow: Seven Studies in Literature.* Reprint. Athens: Ohio University Press, 1997.

NOTES

31   "believed that people were born": Ibid., 97.

31   "Today a man only talks freely": Isaac Babel, in Ilya
        Ehrenburg, *Memoirs*, 425.

31   "has told me many times": Isaac Babel, in Pirozhkova, 79.

32   "endowed with great goodness": Pirozhkova, 1.

32   "Children have been buying": Sergei Eisenstein, in Maria
        Seton, *Sergei M. Eisenstein*, 388.

33   "After Babel's arrest": Pirozhkova, 116.

33   "sealed Babel's room": Ibid., 114.

33   "but even my dresses": Ibid., 117.

34   "I so much wanted": Ibid., 119.

34   "If I mentioned that": Ibid., 141.

35   "made Babel a dark-green": Ibid., 139.

35   "black vinyl sofa": Ibid., 140.

36   "in his native land": Ibid., 171.

CHAPTER ONE: THE HEADLESS MAN

37   "Breughel-like bulk": Lionel Trilling, introduction to *The
        Collected Stories of Isaac Babel*, 21.

37   "Ever since my schooldays": Konstantin Paustovsky, *Years of
        Hope*, 118.

38   "and shared in their legend": Ibid., 121.

38   "Swarming round him": Ibid., 120.

40   "one of the prettiest": Nathalie Babel, introduction to *The
        Lonely Years*, xiii.

41   "our highly original tongue": Isaac Babel, *The Lonely Years*,
        366.

41   "to feed his soul": Pirozhkova, 106.

44   "You are a born intelligence man": Maxim Gorky, in
        Pirozhkova, 44.

45   "it was in the peculiar": Patricia Carden, *The Art of Isaac
        Babel*, 4–5.

46   He could be taciturn: Milton Ehre, *Isaac Babel*, 18.

51   "We met in the foyer": Isaac Babel, *The Lonely Years*, 277.

51   "For the man of spirit": Edmund Wilson, *The Wound and the
        Bow*, 14.

53 "A graceless, puffy-cheeked": Nathalie Babel, introduction to *The Lonely Years,* xiv.

54 "When I start eating cake": Isaac Babel, in ibid., xv.

54 "There could be no question": Paustovsky, 130.

CHAPTER TWO: THE HEADLESS MAN, PART II

59 "Through the years": Jorge Luis Borges, in Richard Burgin, *Conversations with Jorge Luis Borges,* 144.

60 "I went to see": Isaac Babel, in James E. Falen, *Isaac Babel,* 19.

CHAPTER THREE: KIRIL LYUTOV

73 "The special effect": Carden, 203.

78 "basic heartlessness": Richard William Hallett, *Isaac Babel,* 101.

78 "as a real writer": Frank O'Connor, "The Romanticism of Violence," in *The Lonely Voice,* 193.

78 "been dealt a blow": Carden, 134.

80 "I have been criticized": Ilya Ehrenburg, in Isaac Babel, *You Must Know Everything,* 235.

81 "a soldier on reconnaissance": Paustovsky, 126.

CHAPTER FOUR: ARGAMAK

86 "Don't overdo it, Yura": Lev Nikulin, "Years of Our Life," 239.

87 "found himself a character": Carol J. Avins, introduction to *1920 Diary,* xxxii.

91 "fat, pink cigarettes": Paustovsky, 123.

91 "16,000 active sabers": Avins, p. xxii.

93 "Instead of a unitary character": Saul Bellow, "Where Do We Go from Here: The Future of Fiction," 211.

CHAPTER FIVE: BENYA KRIK

98 "Freaks was a thing": Diane Arbus, *Diane Arbus,* 3.

99 "Babel's Cossacks are all": Viktor Shklovsky, "Isaac Babel," 13.

99   "a Jewish Cossack": Raymond Rosenthal, "The Fate of Isaac Babel," 29.

101   "Odessa presents an appearance": Patricia Hurlihy, *Odessa,* 309.

103   "an imaginary town": Nikulin, 246.

104   "Moscow plunged into a life": Radzinsky, *Stalin,* 170.

104   "high forehead, huge head": Shklovsky, 9.

104   "The city was": Ibid., 10.

105   "[had] been beaten": Ibid., 11.

105   gray as a siskin: Ibid., 14.

106   "with a pleasant husband": Nathalie Babel, afterword to *The Complete Works of Isaac Babel,* 1042.

106   "He would dissimulate": Nathalie Babel, introduction to *The Lonely Years,* xxi.

107   "[Babel] has asthma": S. J. Grigorev, in Carden, 18.

111   "spent all his time": Nadezhda Mandelstam, *Hope Against Hope,* 321.

112   "What I am going through": Isaac Babel, in Hallett, 8.

112   "great breaking point": Simon Markish, "The Example of Isaac Babel," 44.

112   "Comrade Budenny has pounced": Maxim Gorky, in Isaac Babel, *The Lonely Years,* 385.

113   "has no parallel": Ibid., 388.

113   *"Red Cavalry* is not": Joseph Stalin, in Carden, 27.

113   "I want to show": Isaac Babel, in Pirozhkova, 107.

115   "engineers, jockeys": Ilya Ehrenburg, "The Wise Rabbi," 69.

115   "his days were like": Ibid., 74.

115   "As long as": Isaac Babel, in Ehre, 27.

CHAPTER SIX: MAKHNO AND MAUPASSANT

117   "Being Russian, French": Nathalie Babel, afterword to *The Complete Works of Isaac Babel,* 1049.

119   "wild, ferocious": Hallett, 32.

122   "I left Russia mostly": Evgenia Babel, in Nathalie Babel, afterword to *The Complete Works of Isaac Babel,* 1041.

124   "On his first visit": Nikulin, 240.

124   "It would be fascinating": Isaac Babel, in ibid., 241.

124   "How nice it would be": Isaac Babel, in ibid., 242.

125   "I lead a most simple life": Isaac Babel, in Carden, 23–24.

125   "[I]t is clear that settling down": Nikulin, 256.

125   "Here [in Paris] a taxi driver": Isaac Babel to Yuri Annenkov, in Isaac Babel, *The Complete Works of Isaac Babel,* 25.

125   "I can't sleep nights": Isaac Babel, in Nikulin, 241.

125   "I am poisoned by Russia": Isaac Babel, in Hallett, 60.

126   "Russia was tiresome": Ehre, 141.

127   "I'm going there to meet": Isaac Babel, in Pirozhkova, 2.

128   "Man lives for the pleasure": Isaac Babel, in Ehrenburg, "The Wise Rabbi," 73.

129   "was a sad person who": Ehrenburg, "Moscow Commemoration of Babel's Seventieth Birthday," 231.

129   "I'm glad I'm going to Moscow": Isaac Babel to Annenkov, in Isaac Babel, *The Complete Works of Isaac Babel,* 25.

129   "My native land": Isaac Babel, in Ehre, 28.

130   "But it's not enough for him": Ehrenburg, "The Wise Rabbi," 75.

130   "For us now the USSR": André Gide, in Vitaly Shentalinsky, *Arrested Voices,* 39.

131   "like horseshoes at the head": Osip Mandelstam, in Nadezhda Mandelstam, *Hope Against Hope,* 13.

133   "But where will the artist": Alexander Blok, in Shentalinsky, 284.

CHAPTER SEVEN: FINAL FICTION

139   "people were opening up": Nadezhda Mandelstam, *Hope Against Hope,* 277.

140   "about whose protracted silence": Georgy Munblit, "Reminiscences of Babel," 268.

140   "I'll breathe more easily": Isaac Babel, in Pirozhkova, 58.

140   "guided by a strategy": Ehre, 25.

140 "His life centered on writing": Nathalie Babel, introduction to *The Lonely Years*, xvii.

140 "I am a Russian writer": Isaac Babel, *The Complete Works of Isaac Babel*, 27.

141 "And that's what I'll call it": Isaac Babel, in Pirozhkova, 111.

141 "the manuscripts confiscated": Isaac Babel, in Shentalinsky, 61.

142 "I'm not afraid of arrest": Isaac Babel, in Pirozhkova, 103.

142 "carrying so many boxes": Pirozhkova, 92.

144 "terrifying and playful labyrinth": Gregory Freidin, "Fat Tuesday in Odessa," 199.

144 "an unknown tongue": Carden, 237.

146 "Terror," she tells us, "was planned": Nadezhda Mandelstam, *Hope Against Hope*, 340.

146 "M. always said": Ibid., 363.

147 "He can't forget her": Pirozhkova, 75.

147 "We were all the same": Nadezhda Mandelstam, *Hope Against Hope*, 340.

148 "morbidly curious about": Ibid., 147.

148 "Why is it": Ibid., 203.

148 "Gorky's a proud man": Stalin, in Radzinsky, 261.

148 "The writers exceed": Nadezhda Mandelstam, in Shentalinsky, 187.

149 "[B]ecause I was homeless": Nadezhda Mandelstam, *Hope Against Hope*, 136.

149 "Peasants just lay quite still": Ibid., 185.

149 "After 1937 people stopped": Ibid., 74.

149 "a prison ward": Ibid., 55.

149 "was played not by terror": Ibid., 126.

150 "the style of our period": Isaac Babel, *The Lonely Years*, 398.

150 "had the courage to say": Gleb Struve, in Isaac Babel, *You Must Know Everything*, 219.

153 "I make my way": Isaac Babel, *The Lonely Years*, 157–58.

153 "since, for old": Ibid, 181.

154 "the dawn of his brief": Nadezhda Mandelstam, *Hope Against Hope*, 322.

155 "a small man": Radzinsky, 259.

156 "Socialist Realism is Rembrandt": Shentalinsky, 258.

156 "You rough fellows do not realize": Gorky, in ibid., 261.

157 "Baudelairean predilection": Gorky, in Isaac Babel, *The Complete Works of Isaac Babel*, 754.

158 "If I were a poet": Stalin, in Radzinsky, 301.

159 Stalin condemns Shostakovich's opera: Ehrenburg, *Memoirs*, 326.

159 "Now they are not": Isaac Babel, in Pirozhkova, 103.

160 "frightened of meeting him": Robert Conquest, *The Great Terror*, 15.

161 "Kolya darling, I earnestly beg you": Evgenia Yezhova, in Radzinsky, 417.

161 "There isn't a single": Conquest, 300.

162 "Again and again": Isaac Babel, *The Lonely Years*, 334.

163 Budenny doesn't believe her: Radzinsky, 387.

164 "and the slightest indiscretion": Nathalie Babel, in Isaac Babel, *You Must Know Everything*, 205.

164 "I aim at a reader": Isaac Babel, in ibid., 220.

164 "I feel like a living corpse": Yezhova, in Marc Jansen and Nikita Petrov, *Stalin's Loyal Executioner*, 170.

164 "Everything that Maupassant": Isaac Babel, in Pirozhkova, 161.

165 "The worst part of this": Isaac Babel, in ibid., 113.

165 "of an important Chekist": Nadezhda Mandelstam, *Hope Against Hope*, 5.

166 "If you are fundamentally flawed": Isaac Babel, in Shentalinsky, 51.

167 "Salvation came to me": Isaac Babel, in ibid., 61.

168 "bottomless grave number 1": Radzinsky, 345.

168 "Tell Stalin that I shall die": Nikolai Yezhov, in ibid., 418.

168 "Even in death she is here": Shentalinsky, 70.

169 And Budenny, on his white horse: Radzinsky, 468.

BABEL'S BRIDE

174 "I told him that my mother": Nathalie Babel, afterword to *The Complete Works of Isaac Babel*, 1027.

174 "We were homeless": Ibid., 1034.

174 "It has remained": Ibid., 1035.

177   "He was a clever performer": Shentalinsky, 35.

177   "Soviet writers when they arrived": Isaac Babel, in ibid., 41.

177   "It was not only in his": Ehrenburg, "The Wise Rabbi," 74–75.

178   "Yezhov is only the instrument": Isaac Babel, *You Must Know Everything*, 232.

178   "and was now living": Nathalie Babel, afterword to *The Complete Works of Isaac Babel*, 1036.

179   "Soviet plants": Ibid., 1040.

179   "had been divorced": Ibid., 1041.

179   "What I do know": Ibid.

180   "In spite of my reluctance": Ibid., 1051.

181   "I saw a woman": Nathalie Babel, introduction to *The Lonely Years*, xxii.

182   "Ehrenburg undoubtedly considered": Nathalie Babel, afterword to *The Complete Works of Isaac Babel*, 1048.

182   "He understood the Revolution": Ehrenburg, "The Wise Rabbi," 75.

183   "Creativity does not dwell": Isaac Babel, *The Lonely Years*, xxiv.

AFTERWARD

188   "with a pugnacious nose": Dan Levin, *Stormy Petrel*, 66.

188   "Like a rocket": Ibid., 80.

189   "It is to books": Gorky, in ibid., 190.

189   "culture's psalm-singer": Leon Trotsky, in ibid., 190.

189   "The bourgeoisie kill": Grigori Zinoviev, in ibid., 198.

189   "but its excrement": Lenin, in Shentalinsky, 229.

190   "would not bite": Levin, 205.

190   "There is something frightening": Gorky, in Shentalinsky, 229.

190   "Alexey Maximovich": Lenin, in Levin, 208.

190   "dining on diamonds": Gorky, in Shentalinsky, 229.

190   "Mary Pickford": Ibid., 244.

190   "We are engaged in trifles": Ibid., 273.

191   "His laconism is": Gorky, in Carden, 191.

192   "After every story": Hallett, 21.

INDEX

Italicized numbers refer to photographs.

About the Author

JEROME CHARYN is the author of more than thirty books, including *Darlin' Bill*, which received the Rosenthal Award from the American Academy and Institute of Arts and Letters. His latest novel, *The Green Lantern*, was a finalist for the 2004 PEN/Faulkner Award. He is a frequent contributor to *Le Monde* and the City section of *The New York Times*. He lives in New York and Paris, where he is Distinguished Professor of Film Studies at the American University.